THE KINGDOM
WARRIOR

THE KINGDOM
WARRIOR

FULL-SPECTRUM SPIRITUAL WARFARE PART 1:
Biblical Clearing and Maintaining Your Spiritual Perimeter

DR. MICHAEL LAKE

Best-selling author of *The Kingdom Priesthood*

DEFENDER

CRANE, MO

*The Kingdom Warrior: Full-Spectrum Spiritual Warfare for the
Remnant in the Last Days*
The Kingdom Paradigm Series, Book Two
By Dr. Michael Lake

Defender Publishing
Crane, MO 65633

ISBN: 978-1-94801468-7

Printed in the United States of America.

A CIP catalog record of this book is available from the Library of
Congress.

Cover design by Jeffrey Mardis
Interior design by Pamela McGrew

Unless otherwise noted, all Scripture quotations are taken from the New
King James Version, © 1982, Thomas Nelson Publishing, Nashville, TN.

This book is dedicated to those who want to be free
and used by God in the last days.

CONTENTS

CONTENTS

INTRODUCTION

Flowing from Genesis to Revelation, the theme of the Kingdom of God slowly builds within the narrative of the Bible. We see glimpses of the Kingdom and its blessings originally in the life of Adam, then through the patriarchs; then it was reestablished by Moses, and we can track it through the reigns of King David and Solomon. Finally, the prophets of Israel foresaw a day coming in which the Kingdom of God would be fully released upon the earth through the reign of the Messiah. Isaiah declared:

> It shall come to pass in that day that the LORD will punish on high the host of exalted ones, and on the earth the kings of the earth. They will be gathered together, as prisoners are gathered in the pit, and will be shut up in the prison; after many days they will be punished. Then the moon will be disgraced and the sun ashamed; for the LORD of hosts will reign on Mount Zion and in Jerusalem and before His elders, gloriously. (Isaiah 24:21–23)

In this powerful prophetic word of Isaiah, the principality wars have come to their inevitable conclusion with the fulfillment of Psalm 82. The rebel members of the Almighty's Divine Council are defeated and brought to justice. John Oswalt, a noted biblical scholar, confirms the subjects of this divine judgment in *The New International Commentary* on the book of Isaiah:

> *The host of the height* is an expression used both for the stars (Jer. 33:22; Neh. 9:6) and for the pagan pantheon, since the gods were frequently identified with the stars (e.g., 2 Chr. 33:5). In late OT and inter-testamental times the pantheon, as the hosts of heaven, was integrated into Hebrew thought as being rebellious angels who came to constitute the spiritual powers at war with God and with his people. It was also understood that certain angels were designated as patrons of nations.[1]

These fallen immortals will one day be defeated and brought to justice. But then, Isaiah announces, like the proverbial icing on the cake, the luciferian elite will be judged with their supernatural cohorts in this cosmic conspiracy. Isaiah also declares that, during the Millennial Reign:

> ...the mountain of the LORD's house shall be established on the top of the mountains, and shall be exalted above the hills; and all nations shall flow to it. **Many people shall come and say, "Come, and let us go up to the mountain of the LORD, to the house of the God of Jacob; He will teach us His ways, and we shall walk in His paths." For out of Zion shall go forth the law, and the word of the LORD from Jerusalem.** He shall judge between the nations, and rebuke many people; they shall beat their swords into plowshares, and their spears into pruning hooks; nation shall not lift up sword against nation, neither shall they learn war anymore. (Isaiah 2:2–4, emphasis added)

I don't feel that our modern theology adequately emphasizes the Millennial Reign of Messiah. Not only is the subject overlooked, but it is flat-out denied by many in the Body of Christ today. Yet, there are more Old Testament prophecies regarding the Second Coming of Christ as

Messiah ben David (the Conquering King) and His reign than there are regarding His First Coming as Messiah ben Joseph (the Suffering Servant). There is a stirring within my spirit to see Jesus sitting on the throne of David in Jerusalem. I have tired of the political corruption in Washington, DC, and the United Nations, and among the technocratic overlords of the Internet. During the reign of Christ, war and conflicts will cease. The earth will experience its Sabbath of rest under the rule of Almighty God, who will have come in the flesh. During this time of unprecedented peace and prosperity, Jesus will teach the nations how to walk in God's judgments, statutes, and commandments.

> Now it shall come to pass in the latter days that the mountain of the LORD's house shall be established on the top of the mountains, and shall be exalted above the hills; and all nations shall flow to it. **Many people shall come and say, "Come, and let us go up to the mountain of the Lord, to the house of the God of Jacob; He will teach us His ways, and we shall walk in His paths." For out of Zion shall go forth the law, and the word of the Lord from Jerusalem.** He shall judge between the nations, and rebuke many people; they shall beat their swords into plowshares, and their spears into pruning hooks; nation shall not lift up sword against nation, neither shall they learn war anymore. (Isaiah 2:2–4, emphasis added)

We must also realize that the Kingdom accompanied Jesus in His First Coming, as outlined in the Gospels. The Messiah-King and His Kingdom are inseparable! Initially, Jesus preached a message of repentance because the Kingdom of God was at hand:

> Now after John was put in prison, Jesus came to Galilee, preaching the gospel of the kingdom of God, and saying, "The time is fulfilled, and the kingdom of God is at hand. Repent, and believe in the gospel." (Mark 1:14–15)

In Mark 1:14–15, the main message Jesus preached during His earthly ministry was one of repentance and preparation for the arrival of God's Kingdom. As I have meditated on the ministry of Jesus over the years, I've often wondered how the modern church would receive His message. Would Jesus be allowed to speak at conferences and mega-churches or be permitted on Christian television? Would the techno-cratic dictators of Facebook (now Meta), Twitter, YouTube, and Google release their army of so-called fact-checkers to censure and ultimately de-platform the King of Glory for producing "hate speech"? I think you already know the answer to these perplexing questions. So, is there any wonder Jesus announced the following to His disciples?

> I tell you that He will avenge them speedily. Nevertheless, when the Son of Man comes, will He really find faith on the earth? (Luke 18:8)

The Greek word Luke used for "faith" in this verse is *pistis* (pis'-tis). *The Enhanced Strong's Lexicon* (*EStrongs*) defines *pistis* as "convic-tion of the truth of anything, belief; in the NT of a conviction or belief respecting man's relationship to God and divine things, generally with the included idea of trust and holy fervour born of faith and joined with it."[2] In *The Kingdom Priesthood*, I drilled down into the lexicons to reveal that this ancient Greek word also means "faithfulness or fidelity." However, considering our discussion, the basic definition of "a convic-tion of the truth of anything" will serve us well. We're in an era of the predominance of personal truth that has no connection to reality what-soever. Questioning someone's "personal" truth, no matter how obscure or delusive, is met with a hate-filled army of social justice warriors (who are neither social nor interested in justice) within the public arena. Find-ing *real* truth in a communistic, "woke" society is as rare as discovering a pirate's chest of gold in one's backyard!

There are two opposing supernatural movements in the world today.

First, the luciferian elite have cast their hellish techno-sorcery spell upon the unregenerate souls of humanity to create an army of angry zombie drones who are impervious to logic, truth, or even rational discussion. This delusional mob is known as "the woke." The other group has been supernaturally awakened by the Holy Spirit. These stirred-up Christian souls are known as the Remnant—those who are characterized by an insatiable appetite for God's truth, His presence, and His manifested Kingdom. With the lines in this conflict firmly drawn, let us return to our discussion of Jesus and the Kingdom.

There are several transitions regarding the Kingdom in Jesus' earthly ministry. First, Jesus declared that repentance was needed because the Kingdom was approaching. Then, Messiah commissioned His disciples to minister and announce that the Kingdom of God has come near to the people:

> And heal the sick there, and say to them, "The kingdom of God has come near to you." (Luke 10:9)

At this point, Luke 10 details the commissioning of the seventy to go forth among God's people. Seventy was not just an arbitrary number of how many disciples Jesus could muster together in His ministry. The number was prophetically strategic in that it's directly related to the Tower of Babel. We discover in Deuteronomy 32:8–9 that God divided the nations among the fallen members of His Divine Council.

> When the Most High gave to the nations their inheritance, when he **divided mankind, he fixed the borders of the peoples according to the number of the sons of God.** But the LORD's portion is his people, Jacob his allotted heritage. (Deuteronomy 32:8–9, ESV; emphasis added)

In *The Kingdom Priesthood,* I documented the following about "God's Strategic Judgment at the Tower of Babel":

At the judgment of God in the Tower of Babel incident, several things occurred. First, the priesthood of darkness, along with their knowledge, was splintering into many groups. Moses told us in Deut. 32:8–9 that this separation was established according to the number of the sons of God. This number varies in both Christian and occult traditions to either 70 or 72. The number seventy is drawn from the number of descendants of Noah outlined in Genesis 10.

Within Talmudic traditions, 72 languages are counted in addition to the 70 nations.[3]

The commissioning of the seventy was Jesus' first significant salvo in His ministry against the principalities and powers that had enslaved humankind. With every changed heart, every healed body, and every soul freed from demonic inhabitation, it was facilitated by a simple drive-by (if you will) of the Kingdom of God. Just passing near someone in bondage, the Kingdom possessed enough power to bring freedom and healing to the prisoners of darkness.

Oh, how we need the Kingdom to come near in this day! No wonder Jesus taught us to cry out daily, "Your Kingdom come!" (Matthew 6:10). Let that cry for the Kingdom's return be established in the heart of every believer today. Let us cry and groan for the Kingdom until it is fully manifested in our midst!

In Luke 17:20–21, Jesus announces:

Now when He was asked by the Pharisees when the kingdom of God would come, He answered them and said, "The kingdom of God does not come with observation; [21] nor will they say, 'See here!' or 'See there!' **For indeed, the kingdom of God is within you.**" (Luke 17:20–21, emphasis added)

The Greek word used by Luke for within is *entos* (*en-tos*). *A Concise Greek-English Dictionary of the New Testament* defines *entos* as "within, in the midst of, among; what is inside, contents (of a cup)."[4] The fact that this word can be translated as both "inside" and "in the midst of" explains the variance between the KJV and many modern translations. I love how the Amplified Bible combines the full definition in its translation.

> Nor will people say, Look! Here [it is]! or, See, [it is] there! For behold, the kingdom of God is within you [in your hearts] and among you [surrounding you]. (Luke 17:21, AMP)

The goal of all Kingdom warriors is to have the Kingdom manifesting both within them and surrounding them at all times. The concept of the presence of the Kingdom both within and around is paramount in Kingdom warfare. The true and ultimate goal of all spiritual warfare is to manifest the Kingdom and see souls delivered from the clutches of the forces of darkness. The Apostle Paul reminds us of this powerful truth in his epistle to the believers in Colossae:

> He has delivered us from the power of darkness and conveyed us into the kingdom of the Son of His love, in whom we have redemption through His blood, the forgiveness of sins. (Colossians 1:13–14)

In our redemption through Christ, a change of spiritual leadership was wrought. From the moment we were born again, we were no longer under the jurisdiction of the principalities and powers that govern the carnal world around us. Instead, we have been conveyed (or translated) into another domain: the domain of the Messiah.

(It would be remiss of me here not to point out that only the new person in Christ is under the domain of Jesus. The old person is still conditioned to listen to the old taskmasters of darkness. Our work in the priesthood crucifies our old nature and teaches us to live by the Spirit and the new person. Only the new person can walk in the Kingdom.)

In our generation, the concept of having the Kingdom of God manifesting both within and around might seem to be an unreachable aspi-
ration. However, when we read the book of Acts, we see the reality of the
Kingdom on every page. I believe the book of the Acts of the Holy Spirit
is still being written today. It continues to be written by the remnant
in every generation since the early Church. The truth is that the most
exciting chapters still lie ahead of us and are woven into the prophetic
tapestry of the final generation before the Lord's return.

We have a daunting task before us. Only through the empowering of the Holy Spirit can we hope to imagine the Kingdom manifesting within and around us. What does the Kingdom contain? How is
the Remnant to transition from the influence of Babylon to becoming
Kingdom-centric? These are just some of the questions I hope to examine more fully in the pages of this book. May the Holy Spirit endow
me with His supernatural grace to set myself aside and allow my King
to write through me as we explore the development of the Kingdom
warrior!

WHERE WE ARE NOW

An Honest Survey

> Be sober, be vigilant; because your adversary the devil walks about like a roaring lion, seeking whom he may devour. Resist him, steadfast in the faith, knowing that the same sufferings are experienced by your brotherhood in the world.
>
> 1 PETER 5:8–9

Our enemy walks through the earth and our lives as a hungry lion. Peter uses a generic word for the enemy because he isn't just referring to Lucifer or Satan, but to all the fallen hordes of Hell. The fallen immortals (fallen angels) and the demonic offspring of the Watchers (Nephilim/demons) remain hungry with an ever-present hatred for the Creator and humankind. These denizens of darkness are never satiated and are constantly seeking an inroad for their task of destruction. Because of this constant hunger of the enemy, the Apostle Peter uses two critical Greek words to be our response in 1 Peter 5:8. These words are "sober" and "vigilant." Let's first examine the word "sober."

A Greek-English Lexicon of the New Testament and Other Early Christian Literature defines "sober" as "to be free from every form of mental and spiritual 'drunkenness', from excess, passion, rashness, confusion, etc., **be well-balanced, self-controlled.**"[5] I find this definition very important, considering the present state of the Church. The priesthood of darkness and its malevolent masters are constantly working behind the scenes to bring mental and spiritual drunkenness into society and the Body of Christ.

The Whore of Babylon is pictured in the Holy Writ as a woman with a goblet filled with an intoxicating wine that is empowered by the very gates of Hell. In the time of judgment, Revelation 18:3 declares:

> For all the nations have drunk of the wine of the wrath of her fornication, the kings of the earth have committed fornication with her, and the merchants of the earth have become rich through the abundance of her luxury. (Revelation 18:3)

In his seminal tome for the *New International Bible Commentary on the Book of Revelation*, Robert H. Mounce notes that judgment falls "because [the Whore] has made the nations drink the maddening wine of her adulteries. Adultery is a well-known figure in the OT for apostasy from God."[6] For the observant believer, it is no surprise that we find ourselves in a neopagan revival among the Western nations. From international corporations to world leaders, we are seeing indications of the maddening wine of Babylon in their statements on the world stage and in their policies. In the days ahead, we will see the construction of the modern-day Tower of Babel and the renewed war against the Creator God. The so-called Great Reset being espoused by the World Economic Forum may very well be the next salvo in this ancient conflict with a humanity that has rejected the leadership of Almighty God. Now let's examine the symptomology of the poisonous vino of the Great Whore.

Many spiritual truths are reflected in the physical world. During His earthly ministry, Jesus would use a grain of wheat or another physical object to illustrate a spiritual reality. Similarly, we can see spiritual truths in the use of *pharmakia* (mind-altering drugs used in sorcery; see Revelation 18:23) and alcohol. A downward spiral is associated with the use of illicit drugs and alcohol. There are many warnings within the Word of God regarding the use and abuse of these substances. This inherently embedded downward spiral looks something like this:

- A warm, fuzzy feeling
- Excitement/euphoria
- A sense of invulnerability
- Intoxication
- Seduction
- Compromise
- Loss of all morality
- Complete addiction

Once the addiction stage is reached, those under a substance's influence will sacrifice anyone or anything for another fix.

What is true in the natural is true in the spiritual. Those who drink from the cup of Mystery Babylon will follow the same downward spiral until they are entirely at the mercy and control of its dark overlords. This addiction can cover all aspects of life, including:

- Financial
- Political
- Religious
- Intellectual
- Physical (to include sexuality)

There is another correlation between the natural and spiritual that we should address at this point. After an initial period of use, more potent doses are required to maintain the same effects upon the user (the drawing vacuum of the downward spiral). For example, marijuana has the reputation of being a "gateway" drug. While many users may start by smoking an occasional joint, they eventually find themselves in the clutches of much more dangerous drugs. The same is true in the occult world. White magic and Freemasonry serve as both a gateway and a recruiting ground for black magic and the depths of perversion in the pagan world. In the shadowy chambers of the occult, the most horrid practices of sexual perversion (inflicted on their victims) and human sacrifice are considered tools of the trade necessary to bring about changes in the physical world. The Apostle Paul reminds us:

> And have no fellowship with the unfruitful works of darkness, but rather expose them. For it is shameful even to speak of those things which are done by them in secret. But all things that are exposed are made manifest by the light, for whatever makes manifest is light. (Ephesians 5:11–13)

A Possible Modern Example of Intoxication to the Dark Vino

A modern example of the depravity toward the end of a downward spiral may be found in the activities that took place on the infamous Jeffrey Epstein's Island near Saint Thomas, Virgin Islands. Dr. Thomas Horn produced an enlightening video entitled *The Hidden Occultism of Epstein's Orgy Island.* Dr. Horn draws from his extensive understanding of occult symbolism to describe in detail what he saw regarding the temple and other structures on the island. A mysterious pagan temple, the sex trafficking of underage girls, and the presence of many leading movers and shakers in the financial and political world are not a good mixture. This combination fostered untold compromise in the lives of those attending these orgies of occult carnality and ensured the financial and political power to keep the secret activities of this island forever hidden from the public.

As the light of journalistic examination began to draw near Epstein Island, many questioned the express delivery of a self-loading cement mixer to the island. This mixer was rushed to the island just three weeks before the expose of the isle and Epstein's exploits was released. *The Daily Mail* noted:

> Jeffrey Epstein had a $100,000 cement truck shipped express to his Caribbean island three weeks before an expose was published which led to his arrest, DailyMailTV can exclusively reveal.... Epstein was in such a hurry that he paid for the machine up front so it would arrive sooner—even though it meant being responsible if it got damaged in transit.[7]

There has been a great deal of debate regarding the need for this type of commercial cement mixer on the island. Was there an attempt to cover up evidence of crimes under tons of concrete, or was it used for typical (but seemly major) construction? It is intriguing that the 7,600-liter (2,000-gallon) cement mixer only cost $50,000. The express delivery fee was as much as the mixer itself. How many thousands of gallons of cement were poured in those three weeks is unknown. The speed in which this project was carried out suggests the former. *The Vigilant Citizen* seems to agree with my assessment:

> In an interview on SiriusXM, U.S. Virgin Islands Senator Oakland Benta admitted that evidence from Epstein's estate "may have been lost."[8]

Because of the sheer number of high-profile visitors to this Pedophile Island and the thousands of gallons of cement poured in haste, the world may never know what transpired on this billionaire's island.

Epstein Island isn't the only example of possible evil. Over the years, through ministries such as that of the late pastor, author, and speaker Russ Dizdar, victims of mind control have shared the reality of such horrendous, perverted crimes that it would make what might have happened on the island look like a Sunday school picnic.

Evangelicalism: Sipping from the Golden Cup of Babylon

While Revelation 18:3 refers to the world and its system, much of the evangelical world first started with an unknowing sip of the wine of Babylon. Over time, more significant portions of the Church world are drinking deeply from the Whore of Babylon's golden cup of iniquity.

Many of the older denominations (Episcopal, Lutheran, Anglican, Methodist, etc.) have long departed from the Word of God for the doctrine of inclusiveness with those trapped by Mystery Babylon. Instead of presenting the Gospel to set these captives free, they have replaced God's truths with concepts of Marxism and outright paganism. The Church of the Living God is no longer calling for a change in the heart of society; it has compromised too much and is now identifying with fallen humanity rather than with the Risen Savior. This downward spiral into the depths of Babylon has grown to the place where former Christian denominations marked by holiness and the fire of God are now claiming abortion is a sacred responsibility.[9]

More of the evangelical movement is surrendering to New Age beliefs, Marxism, and paganism with each passing month. The Word of God is set aside for the high-sounding half-truths of Babylon that appease the flesh rather than calling for its crucifixion.

A large portion of the charismatic/Spirit-filled movement has abandoned proper biblical interpretation for so-called revelations. These dark revelations are nothing more than repackaged New Age doctrines, Jewish mysticism (Kabbalah), and Masonic teachings. It becomes the new standard for building ministries if it draws in crowds and produces increased offerings.

Where do we run to for shelter? The Baptists? Too many Baptist pastors and seminary presidents are Freemasons. The grace of God and the security of the believer have been pushed outside of their biblical bounds to give way to carnality and iniquity. At the same time, legalism is the day's rule in many Baptistic corners.

How about the Hebrew Roots movement? What started in earnest to reclaim a Hebraic understanding of the Gospel, the Church, and the Kingdom has quickly descended into rabbinic legalism, Talmudic and Kabbalistic teachings, and even the embracing of such concepts as the "flat earth." In some corners of the movement, they begin finding problems with the Apostle Paul, but it always seems that Jesus ends up in their crosshairs of contempt, and the King of Glory is rejected as the only True Messiah. Some even move on to have problems with Moses and dive into the cesspool of atheism.

The priesthood of darkness has been working overtime to corrupt any group or movement that God was using to reach a lost and dying world. So when the Apostle Peter told the Body to be vigilant, it was not a suggestion; it was an apostolic warning!

Before we look for a solution, let's continue with our word study in 1 Peter.

Be Well-Balanced and Have Self-Control

The call to be "sober" is to be well balanced and have self-control. This call to soberness is a call to spiritual maturity. The Apostle Paul tells us that the fivefold ministry was established in the Church to do several specific things:

And He Himself gave some to be apostles, some prophets, some evangelists, and some pastors and teachers, for the equipping of the saints for the work of ministry, for the edifying of the body of Christ, till we all come to the unity of the faith and of the knowledge of the Son of God, to a perfect man, to the measure of the stature of the fullness of Christ; that we should no longer be children, tossed to and fro and carried about with every wind of doctrine, by the trickery of men, in the cunning craftiness of deceitful plotting, but, speaking the truth in love, may grow up in all things into Him who is the head—Christ—from whom the whole body, joined and knit together by what every joint supplies, according to the effective working by which every part does its share, causes growth of the body for the edifying of itself in love. (Ephesians 4:11–16)

Few today realize Paul did not invent the fivefold ministry listed in Ephesians 4:11. These ministries already existed in the synagogue and were offices of service to the Jewish community. Biblically speaking, the first apostle was Moses, and the first one the sages of Israel considered to be a prophet was Abraham (although there is some controversy, as some would see Enoch as the first prophet). There is no indication within Paul's writings that any of these offices would be transitory. From the precise wording found in Ephesians 4, the exact opposite is true. All five of these offices would remain in the Body of Christ until…until what?

- Until we come into the unity of the faith.
- Until we come into the unity of the knowledge of who Jesus is and what He came to accomplish.
- Until we stand as a matured Body (perfect humankind).
- Until we reach the measure of the stature of the fullness of Christ. (Jesus is the standard we must reach.)
- Until we are no longer running after every new doctrine but remain solid in a true biblical faith.

The primary task of those called to the fivefold ministry is to prepare the Body for ministry and bring them into spiritual maturity. According to the Apostle Paul, the standard for maturity is attaining the stature of the fullness of Christ. The majority of Christianity has utterly failed this high and noble calling. Of course, there are exceptions to this rule. Some exceptional ministries have paid a challenging price for maintaining their biblical integrity. The Body must honor these faithful ministers and churches for their tireless dedication: They are worth their weight in gold. The remaining ministries must become conscious of their addiction to Mystery Babylon, repent, and return to the purity of God's Word.

I am not aware of a single time within the scope of Church history that we've ever reached full maturity. The canonization of the Bible didn't bring us to the level Paul describes, as many cessationists have suggested. The Hebrew Scriptures were officially canonized sometime around AD 100. The New Testament was canonized in AD 397. It is interesting to note that even the canonization of the New Testament wasn't without controversy. During the Reformation, Martin Luther wanted to remove several books from the New Testament. His strongest argument was against the book of James, although some historians note that he also had the books of Hebrews, James, Jude, and Revelation in his crosshairs. While his labors did see the removal of the Apocrypha of the Catholic Bible from the Protestant version, I am certainly grateful he had little success in his attempts to edit the New Testament. Where would we be without these critical writings today? In His infinite wisdom, the Almighty knew we would need those books to prepare the Body in our day!

The Necessity of Vigilance

The second important word Peter uses in 1 Peter 5:8 is "vigilance." The Greek word he uses for "vigilance" is *gregoreuo*. According to the *Enhanced Strong's Greek Lexicon*, *gregoreuo* means "to watch, give strict attention to, be cautious, active, to take heed lest through remission and indolence some destructive calamity suddenly overtake one."[10]

Throughout Church history, Peter's warning has proven true. The enemy of our soul waits patiently for the Body of Christ to be lulled into a sense of security and to become at ease in this eternal conflict. In times of affluence, the watchtowers of the Kingdom are abandoned or ignored. The true prophets of God (and their prophetic warnings) are slowly replaced with the false prophets of Baal, who boldly announce that all is well and provide prophetic words of plenty and prosperity. As these tainted prophets and preachers sing the siren song of slumber upon the Body, the enemy slowly advances into the hearts of the people and ministries in which it prospers. The result of this tacit attack is not the strengthening and maturity of the Body, but the drunkenness of the nectar of Babylon. Ezekiel saw what happens to God's people when they are lured away from vigilance and into compliancy.

Prophetic Scriptures, Temporal Echoes, and the State of the Body

In biblical prophetic utterances, temporal echoes of the same patterns can be repeated throughout history. I call these prophetic temporal echoes the "fingerprints of God." We are about to recognize a similar echo of what the prophet Ezekiel saw in his day:

> And the word of the LORD came to me, saying, "Son of man, say to her: 'You are a land that is not cleansed or rained on in the day of indignation.' The conspiracy of her prophets in her midst is like a roaring lion tearing the prey; they have devoured people; they have taken treasure and precious things; they have made many widows in her midst. Her priests have violated My law and profaned My holy things; they have not distinguished between the holy and unholy, nor have they made known the difference between the unclean and the clean; and they have hidden their eyes from My Sabbaths, so that I am profaned among them. Her princes in her midst are like wolves tearing the prey, to shed blood, to destroy people, and to get dishonest gain. Her prophets plastered them with untempered mortar, seeing false visions, and divining lies for them, saying, 'Thus says the Lord GOD,' when the LORD had not spoken. The people of the land have used oppressions, committed robbery, and mistreated the

poor and needy; and they wrongfully oppress the stranger. So I sought for a man among them who would make a wall, and stand in the gap before Me on behalf of the land, that I should not destroy it; but I found no one. Therefore I have poured out My indignation on them; I have consumed them with the fire of My wrath; and I have recompensed their deeds on their own heads," says the Lord GOD. (Ezekiel 22:23–31, emphasis added)

It should be noted that what Ezekiel was describing in this passage is a perfect example of the downward spiral of the cup of Babylon upon the people of God. In this ancient prophet's day, the people of God had turned away from the commandments and ways of God for the wine of Babylon and the worship of the old gods (i.e., fallen angels and Nephilim spirits). When the prophet gave forth his utterance, the people had reached the addiction level of the spiral, and the results were monstrous. Now, let's look at this crucial prophetic cry by the ancient Hebrew prophet.

Most believers today are familiar with Ezekiel 22:30. This powerful verse is plucked out of the chapter as a proof text for the need for intercessory prayer. However, few take the time to examine within this prophetic Word *what God is looking for* in the intercessor. This ancient prophet of Israel was crying out against the overwhelming influence the priesthood of darkness had among God's people. We discover that a balanced teaching of the Word had been replaced with corrupt interpretations that appease the flesh. This perversion of God's Word had reached its occult target: the people could no longer distinguish between what was holy and unholy (what was clean and unclean). These tainted priests were teaching the people to violate God's Law and profane His holy things. The leadership, both in the house of God and in the political realm, had an insatiable appetite for power and money. As the administration goes, so go the people. An entire nation was consumed with sensual pleasure, financial gain at all costs, and the accumulation of power. The result was a nation that was destroying itself.

We can easily see the parallels today, not only in America but in the entire Western world as well. Like the people of God in the time of Ezekiel, America is on the precipice of divine judgment. Most of the Church world is still in the grasp of the techno-sorcery slumber of Babylon and ridicules the watchtower calls of the Remnant to repentance and views the return to biblical truth as extreme. Yet, the priesthood of darkness wants the judgment of God to fall on America. Divine judgment is essential to their nefarious plans. The luciferian elite want America, its Constitution, and its foundational Judeo-Christian ethic expunged from the world stage. Using the doctrine of Balaam, they have labored for over a century to bring America to the brink of divine judgment.

Twofold Ministry of the Remnant

The Remnant's task is to become God's Kingdom warriors at this pivotal point in prophetic history. The pleading of intercession flows on two levels:

They are pleading with Heaven to stay execution of judgment and to pour out grace upon the people to wake up and repent. At the same time, they seek judgment for the dark priesthood that will free God's people from their tacit influence.

They are pleading with the people to return to God's ways and abandon the nectar of Babylon.

We need to add something more difficult than pleading with Heaven and earth in our ministries as Kingdom warriors. We must become "the contrast" to the corrupted new normal. We must become the bright example of living opposite of the world (as we will see later, this is the very definition of being holy). We must exude the Kingdom in every aspect of our lives. While others are devouring and being devoured, we will be protected by Heaven and will always be ready to reach out a hand of love to the perishing. We will softly speak the truth in love while others scream and pound the ground in hate. We will not be given to arguments. Instead, we will manifest the Kingdom. This is what Paul was referring to when he said:

> I was with you in weakness, in fear, and in much trembling. And my speech and my preaching were not with persuasive words of human wisdom, but in demonstration of the Spirit and of power, that your faith should not be in the wisdom of men but in the power of God. (1 Corinthians 2:3–5)

The Remnant must seek the maturity the Apostle Paul referred to in Ephesians 4:11–16. Those within the Remnant will be called to the fivefold ministry. Our end-time mandate is to get it right. We must walk in both humility and spiritual boldness. We cannot look to the ministries around us that have been sipping from the cup of the Whore of Babylon as examples. We must return to the purity of the full counsel of God's Word. Our goal is not to become famous or rich. This holy task is to become a conduit of Heaven to mature the Body, bring biblical balance, and make Jesus' name revered in the earth once more. When we get it right, we inoculate the Body from the seductive advances of Babylon.

Bringing Balance to Spiritual Warfare

Today's book market is flooded with books on spiritual warfare. There are countless seminars, conferences, and reference Bibles dedicated to this subject. We are being taught how to command angels (something Jesus never did in His earthly ministry), ascend into the spirit realm to do combat (i.e., astral projection, which is forbidden in Scripture), and so much more. While such teachings are new and exciting, they appeal implicitly to our flesh. There is a combination of deception and euphoria within the soul of the one who practices such things, but few results are seen in the physical world.

In an honest review, more exotic teachings than ever are being presented today on spiritual warfare, but in the real world, the state of both the Church and the world is growing darker by the day. Are we confusing activity with accomplishment? Is it possible that spiritual warfare is more than what we've been led to believe? What if spiritual warfare involved every single aspect of our lives and our influence upon the culture and societies around us? Is our narrow definition and focus handicapping the Body in this ancient struggle between two kingdoms? If this is the case, it would certainly explain the Body's current state. We have left too many gates unguarded, too many watch towers unmanned. Being a Kingdom warrior encompasses every aspect of life and ministry. The Remnant's task is to return to a full-Body ministry and a full spectrum of warfare with the kingdom of darkness. The enemy is constantly testing our boundaries to discover new vulnerabilities and develop new avenues of attack. Peter portrays Satan as a hungry lion looking for something or someone to devour.

Now, let's go back and examine the rest of Peter's admonition to the Church:

But may the God of all grace, who called us to His eternal glory by Christ Jesus, after you have suffered a while, perfect, establish, strengthen, and settle you. (1 Peter 5:10)

I want us to look at several Greek words used by the Apostle Peter in 1 Peter 5:10: "perfect," "establish," "strengthen," and "settle." We have been through an extended time of suffering. I've heard from many believers over the years who confess that the hell almost started the day they were born, and they are seeking divine assistance to stop the suffering! The good news is that the Remnant is awakening, and now a time of restoration must begin. Now, look at this powerful verse in the Amplified Bible again.

And after you have suffered a little while, the God of all grace [who imparts all blessing and favor], Who has called you to

His [own] eternal glory in Christ Jesus, will Himself complete and make you what you ought to be, establish and ground you securely, and strengthen, and settle you. (1 Peter 5:10, AMP)

The Amplified Bible brings out the implied nuance that Christ Himself will bring about the restoration. It will not be attributed to a person or a movement. The Remnant is being awakened around the world by the sole work of the Messiah and His Spirit on the earth. It was not a specific message like God used through Jonathan Edwards on July 8, 1741, that began a great awakening. Nor was it a localized move of God, such as the great outpouring of the Moravian revival at Herrnhut, Germany, in 1727. God began to stir individuals out of their techno-sorcery slumber of Babylon and placed the desire for the King-dom within them. This heavenly stirring has come in waves over the past two decades.

God's Response to the Situation in Ezekiel 22

Therefore say to the house of Israel, "Thus says the Lord GOD: 'I do not do this for your sake, O house of Israel, but for My holy name's sake, which you have profaned among the nations wherever you went. And I will sanctify My great name, which has been profaned among the nations, which you have profaned in their midst; and the nations shall know that I am the LORD,' says the Lord GOD, 'when I am hallowed in you before their eyes. For I will take you from among the nations, gather you out of all countries, and bring you into your own land. Then I will sprinkle clean water on you, and you shall be clean; I will cleanse you from all your filthiness and from all your idols. I will give you a new heart and put a new spirit within you; I will take the heart of stone out of your flesh and give you a heart of flesh. I will put My Spirit within you and cause you to walk in

My statutes, and you will keep My judgments and do them.'"
(Ezekiel 36:22–27)

The prophetic echoes of Ezekiel 36 (God's answer to Ezekiel 22) are being seen in our day. The Remnant is being awakened, repenting, and cleansing their lives. They are seeking out those who will teach the biblical truths that are in line with what the Holy Spirit has written upon their hearts. There is a longing in the hearts of the Remnant for both the presence of God and the empowerment to walk in His ways. Almighty God will cause the Remnant to revere Him again, which will cause the world to stand up and take notice. The Almighty is moving for the sake of His great name. God is releasing a new spirit and heart within the Remnant: it is the heart of a Kingdom warrior.

This return to biblicity will produce the four things promised by the Apostle Peter: perfection (restoration) for God's purposes, establishment of purpose, strength of soul, and settlement (on the foundation of Christ).

Perfection (Restoration) for God's Purposes

In 1 Peter 5:10, the Apostle Peter uses the Greek word *katartizo* (*kat-ar-tid'-zo*) for "perfect." According to *Enhanced Strong's Greek Lexicon*, *katartizo* has several layers of meaning.

> **Perfect:** 1) to render, i.e., to fit, sound, complete, 1a) to mend (what has been broken or rent), to repair, 1a1) to complete, 1b) to fit out, equip, put in order, arrange, adjust, 1b1) to fit or frame for one's self, prepare, 1c) ethically: to strengthen, perfect, complete, make one what he ought to be.[11]

In this long battle, which has been waged since the first family was created on planet earth, the kingdom of darkness and its minions have wrought much suffering and damage. Yet, the Apostle Peter declares the

Lord Himself will begin to repair the damage and bring us to the place He needs us to be in order to fulfill His purposes. We will not only be restored, but outfitted and equipped for the ministries God has called each of us to complete.

Notice something powerful in Peter's words: "the God of all grace." There is more than just one type of grace. In my studies, I've discovered five types, or aspects of, grace:

1. Unmerited favor
2. Saving grace
3. Transforming grace
4. Empowering grace
5. Enduring grace

While I plan to go into depth regarding these five types of grace in chapter 3, I want you to understand now that there is more to grace than just unmerited favor. We will need all of these graces working in our lives to complete the Kingdom tasks before us. I believe the type of grace referred to in 1 Peter 5:10 is transforming grace. In the transformation, there is restoration.

Mounce's Complete Expository Dictionary of Old & New Testament Words expands our understanding of the Greek word *katartizo* to include "adjust thoroughly; to knit together, unite completely."[12] As I read that definition, the first thing that came to mind was this: Whether we need a spiritual chiropractor or surgeon, God's grace has us covered. No matter how disjointed or broken we have become through the suffering inflicted by the enemy, the God of all grace can bring healing and restoration to the Remnant.

A supernatural refreshing is coming to restore the Remnant—spirit, soul, and body. However, we must be vigilant in seeking the Kingdom (and its King) and in being on guard for the stealth-like working of the enemy to derail this coming empowerment.

2

2

2

2

22

2

Establishment of Purpose

The Greek word Peter used for "establish" is *sterizo*. According to *Enhanced Strong's Greek Lexicon*, *sterizo* means "to make stable, place firmly, set fast, fix, to strengthen, make firm, to render constant, confirm, one's mind." God wants to establish a firmness of purpose to the Remnant: His purpose alone. *A Greek-English Lexicon of the New Testament and Other Early Christian Literature* amplifies this concept of mental consistency and strength; it adds "to cause to be inwardly firm or committed, confirm, establish, strengthen."[13] Those who are inwardly firm and committed to their Kingdom mission are less likely to be led into wild tangents or off theological cliffs.

The Remnant are going to know who they are in Christ and their specific mission in the Kingdom. In the days ahead, it will be just as important to say "no" to even noteworthy endeavors if they are not mission-specific to their established purposes in the earth. If the enemy cannot get us off theologically or spiritually, he will attempt to use other peoples' agendas to derail Kingdom priorities. The most limited resources we have are time and physical strength. (The older we get in our natural existence, the more mindful we are of this reality.)

Strength of Soul

There is an exciting dynamic to the Greek word Peter uses to derive "strength." He uses the word *sthenoo*. This originates from the word *sthenos*, which refers to bodily vigor. However, *sthenoo* refers to strengthening the soul.[14]

Have you noticed that many of the words Peter uses have more to do with the soul than the body? Most of our spiritual warfare involves the mind, will, and emotions. As I detailed in *The Kingdom Priesthood*, the soul corresponds with the Second Heaven and the fallen immortals who once served the Creator. Therefore, if God is going to strengthen the

Remnant for the end-time battle, the soul would require major Kingdom reorientation and reinforcement.

Settlement (on the Foundation of Christ)

The final word Peter uses in this powerful promise is "settle." The Greek word for "settle" is *themelioo,* which means "to lay the foundation, to found, to make stable, and establish."[15] The *Logos 10 Bible Software Definition Sense* feature adds, "**to strengthen ⇔ lay a foundation v.**—to strengthen a personal quality or aspect; conceived of as laying a foundation stone or support."[16]

The foundation stone for the Kingdom is Jesus Himself. As the foundation stone, everything built in the Kingdom must align with Him. The more we become like Jesus, inwardly and outwardly, the clearer His image is established in our hearts. It is at this point that we lose ourselves to discover Him. In this great discovery, we can finally determine who we are (freed from sin and Babylon)! The Apostle Paul declared:

> For whom He foreknew, He also predestined to be conformed to the image of His Son, that He might be the firstborn among many brethren. Moreover whom He predestined, these He also called; whom He called, these He also justified; and whom He justified, these He also glorified. (Romans 8:29–30)

Of course, this is in stark contrast to the cornerstone of Babylon, which is Nimrod. Every aspect of Babylon is designed to force us into conformity with Nimrod. The priesthood of darkness wants us to become nothing more than a uniform brick, with which the son of perdition can rebuild the Tower of Babel. While in the Kingdom, there is individuality through which Christ can show His glory; in Babylon, the uniqueness the Creator established is covered up with the miry clay of iniquity. Then the enemy will convince those within his grasp that the miry clay is their true self. Deception is the standard practice of Mystery Babylon.

This terminology of the cornerstone and foundation takes us back to what the Apostle Paul prayed for in Ephesians 3:

> For this reason I bow my knees to the Father of our Lord Jesus Christ, from whom the whole family in heaven and earth is named, that He would grant you, according to the riches of His glory, **to be strengthened with might through His Spirit in the inner man, that Christ may dwell in your hearts through faith; that you, being rooted and grounded in love, may be able to comprehend with all the saints what is the width and length and depth and height—to know the love of Christ which passes knowledge; that you may be filled with all the fullness of God.** (Ephesians 3:14–19, emphasis added)

It is Christ's indwelling, His being the only cornerstone, that causes us to be rooted and grounded in love. The more we understand the heart of our King, the more we will be filled with Him and established for our Kingdom purposes on the earth.

Prayer

Father, I come to you with the realization that I haven't been as sober and vigilant as I should have been. In so many areas of my life, the enemy has either lulled me into slumber or wounded me into submission. I repent of being at ease instead of being engaged upon the battlefield of this world. I humbly come before you and ask that you would heal and restore me. Give me a warrior's spirit, equip me with your truth, and empower me to walk in your Kingdom in such a way that it will bring glory and honor to your name. Let me be a true reflection of Jesus. I desire to see His image completely restored within me. I ask this in Jesus' name.

Review Questions

1. What did the Apostle Peter mean when he called the Church to be "sober and vigilant" in 1 Peter 5:8?
2. What is the downward spiral of addiction to the wine of Babylon?
3. How does the condition of ancient Israel in Ezekiel's day reflect into today's world (both in the Church and secular society)?
4. What is the twofold intercessory ministry of the Remnant today?
5. What did God promise in Ezekiel 36:22–27; why do we need Him to fulfill it again in the Church today?

SPIRITUAL WARFARE

A Full-Spectrum Understanding

> ...lest Satan should take advantage of us;
> for we are not ignorant of his devices.
>
> 2 CORINTHIANS 2:11

While the Apostle Paul could state the Church in Corinthians was not ignorant of the devices of Satan, I don't believe we could say the same thing about the modern Church. The priesthood of darkness has labored tirelessly to pervert the Gospel, corrupt biblical interpretation, and dumb down the Body of Christ regarding the supernatural and the Word of God. It is time to reclaim our spiritual birthright and return to a full-spectrum understanding of God's Word and the dynamics of spiritual warfare.

Lessons Learned in the Military

I approach spiritual warfare from two perspectives: theologically and militarily. I served for about six years in the United States Army. I wish I could tell you that I was a Ranger, Recon, or served in some other exciting specialty during my military tenure (like my good friend and colleague, Jamie Walden). However, I was involved in the administrative aspects of the military service during the Cold War (i.e., semi-peacetime). I was as deadly with an IBM Selectric typewriter as I was with an M16. During my tours of military service, I was fortunate enough to serve at the command level. Whether I was driving a commander around to meetings (and getting to sit in on the briefings) or preparing briefings behind the scenes for a post or division commander, I learned quite a bit about strategic thinking. I also never missed an opportunity to qualify (or at least fire) new types of weapons. Over the years, I've had many deep theological and strategic discussions with members of the Special Forces. In each of these divinely orchestrated sessions, I discovered something new that could be applied to the spiritual life of a believer.

When I was going through boot camp, I learned that transitioning from civilian life to military life can be jarring for most people. It took about a month for the soldiers in my company to adjust to the shocking changes. In fact, we had one situation in which a husband and wife who had enlisted together went AWOL (absent without leave) within the first few days. However, once I got the hang of marching and learning the various ranks (as well as learning respect for the chain of command), I settled in quickly. The entire military atmosphere was a reassurance for me during my basic training. I had come from an unstable home and never knew what to expect from my stepfather (who later adopted me). To be honest, anything—including doing the right thing—could set him off. In the military, a command was a command. There was an order to everything with an exactness I appreciated. So, I was a little sad for boot camp to end.

As with many red-blooded American males, my favorite part of military training was in the use of weapons. The bigger the bang, the bigger my smile. I loved my M16 rifle. I had received some weapons training before I entered the military, and it did not take long for me to qualify as an expert with my firearm. Later in my military career, a grenade launcher was added to the bottom of my M16. The day I qualified with the launcher at Fort Sill, Oklahoma, was one of the coldest days of that year. All of us had dressed for the temperature, but we were still chilled to the bone. I have to admit that the first time I lobbed a grenade into a fifty-gallon steel barrel from about two hundred meters away, the smile kind of froze on my face. Of course, I also enjoyed the training on throwing grenades, firing LAWS (Light Antitank Weapons), and so forth. The bigger the boom, the greater the joy.

What I found tedious (at first) was setting up base camps and guard duty. Establishing and maintaining a safety zone (although we did get to set up Claymore mines), digging foxholes, and walking guard on the perimeter of the camps were laborious at times. On one occasion, I had a paradigm-shifting discussion with a master sergeant. This seasoned soldier had served several tours of combat duty. He was meticulous in his efforts to guard the perimeter of our area. I remember complaining a little bit about the work it involved, and he offered one of those "come to Jesus" moments. "I don't care how good you are with your weapons or what weapons you have," he said, "if your perimeter is not secure, you can easily be overrun by the enemy and killed." The light came on that day: Securing the perimeter was just as important (if not more so) than the skills I had developed with the weapons of warfare.

The same can be said of the Church today. In the spiritual warfare market, the bigger the bang, the bigger the draw is for the teaching. Today's emphasis, whether on deliverance or dealing with principalities and powers, is all about spiritual weapons. There is little or no instruction about the protocols (rules of engagement) or maintaining a perimeter (hedge of protection). The result of this myopic approach is that the enemy has decimated lives and ministries. For the most part, the Body of Christ is like a city without walls; we have outstanding weapons but no security.

Transferring from stateside service to an overseas posting was as eye-opening as my discussion with that master sergeant. The Third Infantry Division's headquarters (HQ) was a mere twenty minutes away by air from the East German border. Not only did I have to deal with being awakened at zero dark thirty in the morning without warning to rehearse as if we had communist troops on the way, I had to learn the basics regarding espionage. The possibility of covert operators from the enemy infiltrating our ranks was a constant possibility. Infiltration could lead to the operator flipping you and making you an asset for the other side. This conversion could occur through seduction, coercion, or blackmail. While serving in the chief of staff's office, I remember seeing the court martial paperwork on a young man who had unwittingly provided classified information to a female operative posing as his girlfriend. His military career was over, and the seductress had disappeared into the night.

How many believers over the centuries have become the Church's greatest enemies? In our day, I can think of several philosophers/atheists who attack the Church with a fervor only Hell could spawn. These have destroyed the faith of thousands of young Christians attending colleges or universities. In each case, these enemies of the Gospel were once ministers of the Gospel. However, we don't have to go to that extreme. How many so-called believers do we have in congregations today who were seduced or coerced by demonic spirits, and these agents of darkness use their mouths and actions to sow discord among the brethren? Whether through seduction or woundedness, these believers have become assets for the kingdom of darkness.

A Call for Maturity

When I was a young minister back in the 1980s, I was reading a book on deliverance. As I read through the pages, I was taken aback by a story the author shared. While his team was ministering deliverance to an individual, half of his ministerial staff began manifesting demons! From the author's perspective, such occurrences seemed normal, but they shouldn't be. While this particular group understood the authority that resides in the precious name of Jesus, they knew little about cleaning house spiritually or maintaining their hedges of protection.

Over the years, I've seen groups get into various trends within spiritual warfare, such as spiritual mapping. The primary intent of spiritual mapping is to discover the principality, power, or ruler over any area and then engage in battle with these ancient fallen immortals. As I detailed in *The Kingdom Priesthood*, the rules of engagement with Second Heaven entities are entirely different from those of the First Heaven. This misapplication is because too many ministers have lifted Ephesians 6 out of its biblical and historical context. The result has been equivalent to bringing a knife to a gunfight or poking a grizzly bear with a stick. Lives have been lost, families have been destroyed, and ministries have closed. These tragedies became so prevalent that the late minister, author, and teacher John Paul Jackson felt it necessary to publish his book, *Needless Casualties of War*. In this now-classic Christian work, Jackson details the tragedies that can occur when proper protocols are not followed in spiritual warfare. Yet with all the warnings from the seasoned warriors in our ranks, the subject of spiritual warfare is still all about the big boom.

Although I will be dealing with the weapons of our warfare in this book, I'll pay special attention to what few ministries are teaching today. This is not just another book on traditional spiritual warfare. I want to provide you with the information that Mary and I did not have back in the 1990s when all hell came against us. We learned these truths by the grace of God while under extreme fire from the enemy. If these truths had not worked, we would not have survived those attacks.

We approach spiritual warfare from a Greco-Roman mindset. We have believed the lie that we can compartmentalize various aspects of our lives, accepting the illusion that we can separate elements of life as with the food on students' trays in their elementary-school cafeterias. From a Hebraic (i.e., biblical) perspective, life is more like a pie or stew. Everything is mixed and influences everything else added to the pot. There is a psycho-physio-spiritual unity to life. We are tripartite beings. What affects the spirit can affect the mind or flesh, and vice versa. We need to wake up to the fact that every aspect of life—what we think, what we say, and what we do, all of it—has a spiritual warfare component. Even maintaining sound doctrine is a task of spiritual warfare! Oh, how the enemy would love for us to run off into some new trend or tangent he has covertly sown into contemporary theology. These demonic-inspired rabbit trails always end in shipwrecked lives and destroyed ministries. The Apostle Paul would call these things "every wind of doctrine" (Ephesians 4:14–16).

I pray that through this writing you will secure your area of operation (AO), become impervious to infiltration, and mature into the true Kingdom warrior God has called you to be.

In this book, we will be dealing with a more holistic, full-spectrum approach to spiritual warfare. Our concepts of spiritual warfare must include every aspect of life and ministry. We will be exploring:

- ✣ Getting our theologies in line with the Word of God.
- ✣ Learning how to drive the enemy out of our lives and to close the doors he used.
- ✣ Discovering how to establish and maintain our hedges of protection.
- ✣ Adopting a two-prong approach to deliverance: self-deliverance (i.e., sanctification) and the ministry of deliverance for those who need a helping hand.
- ✣ How to become impervious to the covert operations of the enemy.
- ✣ Becoming seasoned sharpshooters with the weapons of our warfare.
- ✣ Finally, becoming a faithful watchers and intercessors in the Kingdom.

As we move forward in this work, please remember the words of that seasoned Army master sergeant: "I don't care how good you are with your weapons or what weapons you have. If your perimeter is not secure, you can easily be overrun by the enemy and killed."

Now, on to a full-spectrum approach to spiritual warfare.

Prayer

Father, my heart's desire is to be an effective warrior for you. Give me to the grace to learn the protocols of spiritual warfare. Warfare is more than weapons; there are tactics and strategies involved. Open my eyes to see and my heart to learn your ways. May I give no place for the enemy in my life, except for the space under my feet as I tread upon his kingdom in your name, in Jesus' name.

Review Questions

1. Why is warfare of any kind (both physical and spiritual) more than just about weapons?
2. Why is keeping our theologies and strategies in line with the Word of God important?

THE FIVE TYPES OR
ASPECTS OF GRACE

But may the God of all grace, who called us to His eternal glory
by Christ Jesus, after you have suffered a while,
perfect, establish, strengthen, and settle you.

1 PETER 5:10

Years ago, I was sitting in my home channel-surfing across some of
the Christian stations we had at that time on satellite. I happened
upon a well-known preacher speaking about grace. The minister was
young and dynamic; from his curated wardrobe to the professionally
designed stage, everything about him exuded prosperity. I had heard
this young man before. His message was on the unmerited favor of God.
This one message served as the cornerstone for everything he preached.
As I listened carefully, I noticed he was cherry-picking certain Scriptures
and avoiding other biblical references that would bring into question his
revelations, then completely lifting verses out of their context to prove
his hypotheses. My heart became grieved at his misuse of specific biblical
references and at his completely ignoring the principles of proper biblical interpretation (hermeneutics).

As I pondered his presentation, I also remembered my early days in

ministry. In the charismatic movement, many who served as examples to
us younger ministers played fast and loose with biblical interpretation.
Inspiration and revelation rather than diligent exegesis were the tools of
the trade used to dig out the pure gold of the Word of God. As I sat there
repenting of my younger years, thanking God for my years in seminary,
and praying for this minister, the Holy Spirit began to speak to my heart.
He took me to 1 Peter 5:10 and showed me there is more to grace than
the unmerited favor of God. This event began a journey of discovery;
as I shared earlier, five types or aspects of grace are revealed in the Bible.

When Peter was penning this powerful promise in 1 Peter 5:10, the
Greek word he used for "all" is *pas*. *A Greek-English Lexicon of the New
Testament and Other Early Christian Literature* (BDAG) states *pas* can
be defined as "to totality with focus on its individual components, each,
every, any."[17] *The Logos Bible Software's Sense* feature presents the definition as: "entire—constituting the full quantity or extent; complete."[18]
While most translations of the Bible render this quote from Peter as "the
God of all grace," the Complete Jewish Bible provides a slight variation:
"God, who is full of grace." Peter understood just how much suffering
the believers in his day endured. This seasoned apostle was praying they
would experience God's grace's full depth. It would take "all grace" to
fulfill his prayer of God perfecting, establishing, strengthening, and set-
tling them. Unfortunately, the Remnant find themselves living in a day
when evil is ascending within the social consciousness of the nations
in which they reside. The old gods of the pagan world are flexing their
muscles of influence once again and have declared war on the God of the
Bible and His people. If there was ever a time when the Remnant needed
the full depth of God's grace, it is now!

The Five Types of Grace Revealed in the Bible

Five types (or aspects) of grace are revealed in the Word of God. Sometimes, the definition can simply be found in the original Hebrew or

Greek word used within the text. At other times, the types of grace are either revealed in the context or in the story itself.

These five types of grace are:

1. Unmerited favor
2. Saving grace
3. Transforming grace
4. Empowering grace
5. Enduring grace

Before we explore these types of grace, I want to examine the word "grace" in the Word of God.

If we search for the word "grace" in the King James Version of the Bible, we'll discover that it is used 148 times in 137 verses. At first blush, it would appear that grace is primarily a New Testament concept, since only eighteen verses in the Old Testament contain the word "grace." However, something completely different begins to appear when we dig into the original language.

Grace in the Old Testament

Let's look at the two primary words in biblical Hebrew that express the concept of "grace": *chesed* and *chen*.

1. *Chesed* means "goodness, kindness, and faithfulness."[19] There are two times in the Hebrew text that the context requires it to be translated as "a reproach, and shame."[20] This Hebrew word is used 248 times in the Old Testament. Here is a breakdown of its usage within the KJV Bible: "mercy"-149; "kindness"-40; "lovingkindness"-30; "goodness"-12; "kindly"-5; "merciful"-4; "favor"-3; "good"-1; "goodliness"-1; "pity"-1; "reproach"-1; and "wicked thing"-1.

2.   *Chen* means "favor, grace, charm, elegance, and acceptance."[21]
     This Hebrew word is used 69 times in the Old Testament.
     Here are the various ways it is translated in the KJV Bible:
     "grace"-38; "favor"-26; "gracious"-2; "pleasant"-1; "precious"-1;
     "well-favored" + Strongs H#02896 1.

These two words combined are used 317 times. However, there are
many examples of the grace of God within the Hebrew text in which
neither *chesed* or *chen* is used. We will examine the first example of this
truth later in this chapter.

Grace in the New Testament

In the New Testament, two words are used for "grace." The first is the
counterpart for the Hebrew *chen*: the Greek *charis*. *Charis* appears 156
times in the original Greek text of the New Testament and is used in
various ways in the New Testament. It means:

1) grace; 1a) that which affords joy, pleasure, delight, sweetness,
charm, loveliness: grace of speech; 2) good will, loving-kindness,
favor; 2a) of the merciful kindness by which God, exerting his
holy influence upon souls, turns them to Christ, keeps, strength-
ens, increases them in Christian faith, knowledge, affection, and
kindles them to the exercise of the Christian virtues; 3) what is
due to grace; 3a) the spiritual condition of one governed by the
power of divine grace; 3b) the token or proof of grace, benefit;
3b1) a gift of grace; 3b2) benefit, bounty; 4) thanks, (for ben-
efits, services, favors), recompense, reward.[22]

In the 156 times it is used, *charis* is translated as "grace 130,
favor 6, thanks 4, thank 4, thank + Strongs G# 2192 3, pleasure

4

2, misc 7." [23] It should also be noted that *charis* is also a part of the word "charisma," which refers to the gifts of the Holy Spirit. Henry G. Liddell's *A Greek-English Lexicon* reveals that "charisma" is a "gift of God's grace."[24]

When the true gifts of the Holy Spirit are manifested within the Body of Christ, they will be saturated in the beautiful grace of God.

The second word used for "grace" in the Greek New Testament is *Eleos,* the Greek counterpart to the Hebrew word *chesed. Eleos* means:

1) mercy, kindness or good will towards the miserable and the afflicted, joined with a desire to help them; 1a) of men towards men: to exercise the virtue of mercy, show one's self merciful; 1b) of God towards men: in general providence; the mercy and clemency of God in providing and offering to men salvation by Christ; 1c) the mercy of Christ, whereby at his return to judgment he will bless true Christians with eternal life.[25]

It is used 28 times in the Greek text and is always translated as "mercy" in the King James Version of the Bible.

Both words combined occur 184 times in the New Testament.

When considering the use of all four words within the original text, the concept of grace is spoken of more in the Old Testament than the New. However, it should be noted that the text of the Old Testament is much larger than that of the New Testament. This makes sense, because from Genesis to Revelation, we are dealing with the same loving, grace-centric God. Now, let's examine the first situation in which the grace of God is exemplified in the Bible. In these verses, God's grace is both hidden in His name and revealed in His actions.

When God Created Humanity

In the beginning God created the heavens and the earth. (Genesis 1:1)

In the Creation narrative, Almighty God is referred to simply as "God." In Hebrew, this word for "God" is *Elohim*. We find something very interesting in the words of the *nachesh* (serpent) in the garden:

Now the serpent was more cunning than any beast of the field which the LORD God had made. And he said to the woman, "Has God indeed said, 'You shall not eat of every tree of the garden'?" (Genesis 3:1)

This fallen seraph only refers to God as *Elohim*. Yet, within the Creation story of Adam and Eve, a new name for God is revealed: *Yahweh-Elohim*.[26] *Yahweh* is known as the tetragrammaton and is considered the most sacred name for the Creator. It appears from the text that this ancient dragon did not know God by this name! Here is what the ancient sages of Israel reveal about God's name as *Yahweh-Elohim*.

The divine appellation *Elohim*, translated "God," was understood to denote His aspect of judgment, and *YHVH*, translated "Lord," His aspect of mercy (Gen. R. XXXIII. 3), and the combination of the two names in the verse, "These are the generations of the heaven and the earth when they were created, in the day that the Lord God (*YHVH-Elohim*) made earth and heaven" (Genesis 2:4) is explained as follows:

It may be likened to a kind who had empty vessels. The king said, "If I put hot water into them they will crack; if I put icy water into them they will contract." What did the king do? He mixed the hot with the cold and poured the mixture into the vessels, and they endured. Similarly said the Holy One, blessed is He, "If I create the world only with the attribute of mercy, sin will multiply beyond all bounds; if I created it only with the attribute of justice, how can the world last? Behold, I will create it with both attributes; would that it might endure!" (Gen. R. XII. 15). Indeed, it was only because the quality of mercy prevailed at Creation that the human race was allowed to come into being.[27]

In other words, *YHVH* represents the mercy or grace of God, and *Elohim* represents His justice or position as Supreme Judge. In the creation of humanity, the Creator/Judge revealed an aspect of Himself that not even the angels knew: This God was a redeemer, full of grace and mercy. The Almighty balanced grace and judgment together perfectly for the only aspect of creation that He would ever move to redeem—humanity. Therefore, every time *YHVH* is used in the Hebrew Bible, it represents the grace of God. This most sacred name for God is used 6,519 times in the Old Testament!

In this powerful name for God, *YHVH-Elohim*, the First and Second coming of Messiah are also revealed. Remember, *YHVH* represents the grace and mercy of God. The first time Jesus came to the earth, He came as the Kinsman Redeemer. Jesus walked the shores of Galilee as *YHVH* in the flesh: He was Messiah ben Joseph (the Suffering Servant). The Apostle John declares in his Gospel:

> In the beginning was the Word, and the Word was with God, and the Word was God. He was in the beginning with God. All things were made through Him, and without Him nothing was made that was made. In Him was life, and the life was the light of men. And the light shines in the darkness, and the darkness did not comprehend it. (John 1:1–5)

John declared in no uncertain terms that the Creator walked among the people, but the darkness in them could not comprehend who He was. John testifies that Jesus was *YHVH* who had come in the flesh. John continued:

> He came to His own, and His own did not receive Him. But as many as received Him, to them He gave the right to become children of God, to those who believe in His name: who were born, not of blood, nor of the will of the flesh, nor of the will of man, but of God. (John 1:11–13)

Why did John say "He came to His own, and His own did not receive Him?" Because it was the preincarnate Christ (YHVH) who revealed Himself to Moses and delivered the Israelites from Egypt. It was Jesus who married Israel around Mount Sinai and gave the commandments to Moses. He (Jesus) was the God of Abraham, Isaac, and Jacob. If any group of people on the planet should have recognized who Jesus was, it should have been the "people of God!"

When we examine the Hebrew word *Yahweh*, we discover that it is comprised of four Hebrew letters: *Yod, Hey, Vav,* and *Hey.* Each has both a meaning and a numeric value. Here are their meanings:

Yod = "hand"

Hey = "behold," "reveal," "window"

Vav = "nail"

Hey = "behold," "reveal," "window"

Thus, this string of ancient Hebrew letters can be interpreted as: "The God with the nailed hand shall be revealed twice."

Another way of referring to the tetragrammaton (*YHVH*) is to say

"I AM." In the teachings of Jesus, He referred to Himself as "I AM." We find this event in the eighth chapter of the Gospel of John.

> Jesus said unto [the Jewish leaders], Verily, verily, I say unto you, Before Abraham was, I am. Then took they up stones to cast at him: but Jesus hid himself, and went out of the temple, going through the midst of them, and so passed by. (John 8:58–59, KJV)

We find in this discussion that the Jewish leaders called Him a "Samaritan" and that He had a demon. The Samaritans were half Jewish and half Gentile, and were hated by the Jewish people during the Second Temple Period. To add insult to injury, they were claiming that Jesus was working miracles in their midst, not as the Messiah, but as someone who was demon possessed. It was at this point in their heated argument that Jesus revealed who He really was: "I AM." At that moment, He declared He was Yahweh who had come in the flesh. This so enraged the people that they rose to kill Him. But, since He was the Creator, who had come in the flesh, and it wasn't time for Him to offer up His life, He simply walked through the crowd and hid Himself from the people.

Why am I belaboring this point about who Jesus is? I. Howard Marshall is professor emeritus of New Testament exegesis at the University of Aberdeen, Scotland. He is also regarded as one of the front-ranking New Testament scholars in the world. In his volume for the *New International Commentary of the New Testament on the Epistles of John*, Dr. Marshall notes:

> But why does the writer say this in such an ambiguous manner? He is thinking of two things, which are nevertheless one. On the one hand, he is thinking of the Christian message which is the object of Christian proclamation and is heard by men; he himself is proclaiming it to his readers so that they may enjoy the blessings which come to those who receive it (v. 3). This message was preached by Jesus himself. On the other hand,

Jesus himself can be described as the Word. The message takes concrete form in him. I may send a girl a message saying that I love her; I can also send her a costly ring which will be immediately recognizable to her as a tangible message of love. Jesus is both the preacher of God's message and the message itself. Paul could say, "**We preach Christ**" (1 Cor. 1:23; cf. 2 Cor. 4:5), **showing that the message and the person are ultimately identical.** Similarly, the writer to the Hebrews can tell how "God spoke to our forefathers through the prophets at many times and in various ways, but in these last days he has spoken to us by his Son" (Heb. 1:1f.). **Our writer here wants to emphasize that the Christian message is identical with Jesus; it took personal form in a person who could be heard, seen, and even touched.**[28] (Emphasis added)

In other words, the Gospel and Jesus are one. If you change who Jesus is, you have changed the Gospel. If you change the Gospel, you have distorted who Jesus is. In today's world, we have to ask, "Which Jesus is the speaker referring to?" There is the Mithra-based Jesus of Constantine. There is the "prosperity Jesus" of the charismatic movement. There is the Jesus of Calvinism about whom the term "whosoever will" is transformed into only those who are predestined. Recently, to the horror of parishioners in the United Kingdom, the new Jesus being preached is transsexual. *The New York Post* reports:

A dean at the University of Cambridge in the UK came to the defense of a junior research fellow whose sermon last Sunday about Jesus Christ having a "trans body" reportedly left outraged congregants "in tears."

   Dr. Michael Banner, the dean of Trinity College, said Joshua Heath raised "legitimate" speculation in his Evensong sermon, during which the researcher claimed from the pulpit of Trinity College chapel that non-erotic portrayals of Jesus' penis in historical paintings "urge a welcoming rather than hostile response towards the raised voices of trans people," according to *The Daily Telegraph*.

"In Christ's simultaneously masculine and feminine body in these works, if the body of Christ as these works suggest the body of all bodies, then his body is also the trans body," Heath said.

Heath, whose PhD in theology was supervised by the former Archbishop of Canterbury Rowan Williams, also claimed that in one of the Medieval paintings he displayed to the congregation, the spear wound in Jesus' side "takes on a decidedly vaginal appearance." In another, he pointed out how the blood from his side flows to his groin.

Heath's homily during the traditional Anglican service left many in attendance, including children, "visibly uncomfortable," according to an anonymous congregant who fired off a complaint letter to Banner. Shouts of "Heresy!" reportedly rang out in the church as incensed worshipers left in disgust.[29]

There should have been shouts of heresy that day. Whenever we change who Jesus is from the biblical narrative, we are creating a false idol to be erected in His place. This false idol produces another gospel that, at best, will destroy someone's faith and, at worst, lead that person into a devil's Hell.

Rediscovering the biblical Jesus will cause us to rediscover the Gospel the Early Church preached. This holy task is the duty of the Remnant in our day.

Now, let's go back to the words of John in John 1.

The apostle continues with an even more powerful revelation: To those who received Him, He gave power (or the right) to become the children of God. The word John used for "power" or "right" is *exousia* in the Greek text. *Exousia* is also employed in a powerful instance when Jesus instructed His discipes regarding spiritual warfare.

Then the seventy returned with joy, saying, "Lord, even the demons are subject to us in Your name." And He said to them, "I saw Satan fall like lightning from heaven. Behold, I give you the authority to trample on serpents and scorpions, and over all the power of the enemy, and nothing shall by any means hurt you. Nevertheless do not rejoice in this, that the spirits are subject to you, but rather rejoice because your names are written in heaven." (Luke 10:17–20)

That day, Jesus was giving His disciples an upgrade in spiritual warfare. The seventy had gone out precisely as Jesus had instructed. Their faithfulness in this matter resulted in Messiah expanding their authority. The Greek word for "authority" in Luke 10:19 is *exousia*. The word He used for the enemy's power is *dunamis*, which refers to supernatural power. In fact, *dunamis* is also used in Acts 1:8.

But you shall receive power when the Holy Spirit has come upon you; and you shall be witnesses to Me in Jerusalem, and in all Judea and Samaria, and to the end of the earth. (Acts 1:8)

John 1:12 could easily be translated:

But as many as received Him, to them He gave the right [authority] to become children of God, to those who believe in His name. (John 1:12)

The primary definition for *exousia* is the "power of choice."[30] To those who believe in Jesus and His completed work, saving grace releases within them the authority to reject the kingdom of darkness and accept Jesus for salvation. Salvation itself is an act of authority!

I know I was supposed to be dealing with the grace of God revealed in His name and how the first family experienced God's unmerited favor. But the truth of God is so overwhelming sometimes that I couldn't help myself. So, before I run down another rabbit trail, let's head back to Genesis 3.

Judgment and Grace in the Garden

Then the LORD God called to Adam and said to him, "Where are you?" So he said, "I heard Your voice in the garden, and I was afraid because I was naked; and I hid myself." And He said, "Who told you that you were naked? Have you eaten from the tree of which I commanded you that you should not eat?" Then the man said, "The woman whom You gave to be with me, she gave me of the tree, and I ate." And the LORD God said to the woman, "What is this you have done?" The woman said, "The serpent deceived me, and I ate." So the LORD God said to the serpent: "Because you have done this, You are cursed more than all cattle, and more than every beast of the field; on your belly you shall go, and you shall eat dust all the days of your life. And I will put enmity between you and the woman, and between your seed and her Seed; He shall bruise your head, and you shall bruise His heel." To the woman He said: "I will greatly multiply your sorrow and your conception; in pain you shall bring forth children; Your desire shall be for your husband, and he shall rule over you." Then to Adam He said, "Because you have heeded the voice of your wife, and have eaten from the tree of which I commanded you, saying, 'You shall not eat of it': Cursed is the ground for your sake; in toil you shall eat of it all the days of your life. Both thorns and thistles it shall bring forth for you, and you shall eat the herb of the field. In the sweat of your face you shall eat bread till you return to the ground, for out of it you were taken; for dust you are, and to dust you shall return." And Adam called his wife's name Eve, because she was the mother of all living. Also for Adam and his wife the LORD God made tunics of skin, and clothed them. (Genesis 3:9–21)

This biblical narrative of the Fall of humanity reveals several important truths, some of which the Church today is utterly ignorant.

Grace, unmerited favor, was extended to Adam and Eve in the Garden. Nevertheless, this hand of grace from Almighty God did not nullify all the consequences of their sin. Although they did not physically die on the spot, the following happened:

- ✤ They were infused with the sin nature (the iniquity force).
- ✤ Eve would experience pain in childbirth. Note: Regardless of what modern feminists in the Church would have us believe, the pronouncement of Eve's desire would only be for her husband, and rule (lovingly) over her was not a judgment; it was a refocusing. In the narrative, before the serpent appeared in the Garden, Eve only knew two voices: that of her husband and that of God. In this narrative, she submitted to a third voice: the serpent's.
- ✤ Adam would now experience sweat and labor in his efforts to produce food for his family.
- ✤ The first family was expelled from the Garden.

For this first couple, there was a stay of execution. Instead, Adam and Eve were promised a Redeemer through the seed of the woman, who would bring the ultimate judgment upon this fallen seraph. We see the complete fruition of this judgment in the book of Revelation, when the dragon is thrown into the Lake of Fire.

Adam and Eve received unmerited favor in the Garden that day and a promise of saving grace through the seed that was to come. The serpent, who only knew God as Elohim, received no grace that day. Judgment alone was pronounced over him: some instantaneous, some progressive, and some prophetic.

Unmerited Favor Leads to Saving Grace

For by grace you have been saved through faith, and that not of yourselves; it is the gift of God, not of works, lest anyone should boast. For we are His workmanship, created in Christ Jesus for good works, which God prepared beforehand that we should walk in them. (Ephesians 2:8–10)

As I read the writings of the Apostle Paul, I stand amazed at the graceful balance in his theology and the symmetry of the concepts he explains as a master theologian and teacher. In these two verses, he expounds on and balances grace, faith, and works.

God's unmerited favor releases saving grace in our lives. That saving grace is accessed through faith in the complete work of Messiah (as well as through the understanding of who He is). This act of faith fulfills the declaration of the Apostle John in John 1:12: Grace gives us the authority to become children of God. Entering salvation is our first action in spiritual warfare. (I believe the second act of spiritual warfare is baptism: it puts Hell on notice that we're now only under the jurisdiction of our new King, Jesus of Nazareth.) Then Paul balances out the concept of righteous works; they belong solely to those who are redeemed. These biblical works, which we are recreated for, are not to gain salvation but are the fruit of that salvation taking hold in our lives: perfect symmetry! Attempts to establish salvation in any other order will short-circuit the entire process and only produce religiosity.

Transforming Grace—Wrestling with God

Then Jacob was left alone; and a Man wrestled with him until the breaking of day. Now when He saw that He did not prevail against him, He touched the socket of his hip; and the socket of Jacob's hip was out of joint as He wrestled with him. And He said, "Let Me go, for the day breaks." But he said, "I will not let You go unless You bless me!" So He said to him, "What is your name?" He said, "Jacob." And He said, "Your name shall no longer be called Jacob, but Israel; for you have struggled with God and with men, and have prevailed." Then Jacob asked, saying, "Tell me Your name, I pray." And He said, "Why is it that you ask about My name?" And He blessed him there. And Jacob called the name of the place Peniel: "For I have seen God face to face, and my life is preserved." Just as he crossed over Penuel the sun rose on him, and he limped on his hip. Therefore to this day the children of Israel do not eat the muscle that shrank, which is on the hip socket, because He touched the socket of Jacob's hip in the muscle that shrank. (Genesis 32:24–32)

In the life of every believer, there will come a night watch in which we end up wrestling with God. I have found from personal experience that there may be small wrestling matches throughout our lives. These are times of the Holy Spirit dealing with our carnal nature. It is usually something we do not want to mortify, but maturing in Christ demands it. However, with the night watch, this wrestling with God is a life-altering event that will define us from that moment forward.

This night watch by the ford of Jabbok was such an event in Jacob's life. The ford of Jabbok is a stream that intersects the mountain range of Gilead and falls into the Jordan on the east, about midway between the Sea of Galilee and the Dead Sea. The word itself means "empty."[31] We usually end up wrestling with God the most in the empty places in our lives where we must come face to face with the consequences of our past. Jacob had usurped (or supplanted) his way to stealing both the firstborn's right and Isaac's blessing for Esau. That is what the name "Jacob" means—the "supplanter" (or "heel holder").[32] God had richly blessed him while he had been living with Laban (and despite Laban). He was returning home with great wealth and a caravan of family and servants. Jacob had sent part of his entourage before him with gifts for

Esau, even referring to himself as "Esau's servant" (Genesis 32:20). This greeting Jacob sent ahead was the exact opposite of what was prophetically spoken over Esau by his father, Isaac.

> Then Isaac answered and said to Esau, "Indeed I have made him your master, and all his brethren I have given to him as servants; with grain and wine I have sustained him. What shall I do now for you, my son?" And Esau said to his father, "Have you only one blessing, my father? Bless me—me also, O my father!" And Esau lifted up his voice and wept. Then Isaac his father answered and said to him: "Behold, your dwelling shall be of the fatness of the earth, and of the dew of heaven from above. By your sword you shall live, and you shall serve your brother; and it shall come to pass, when you become restless, that you shall break his yoke from your neck." (Genesis 27:37–40)

I might add here that Esau later broke free from serving Jacob. The family of Esau became the Edomites. Throughout the Old Testament, the Edomites served the people of God, such as during the life of King David, and eventually they gravitated toward an adversarial role. Obadiah began his prophetic ministry by foretelling the destruction of Edom.

> The vision of Obadiah. Thus says the Lord GOD concerning Edom (We have heard a report from the LORD, and a messenger has been sent among the nations, saying, "Arise, and let us rise up against her for battle"): "Behold, I will make you small among the nations; You shall be greatly despised. The pride of your heart has deceived you, You who dwell in the clefts of the rock, Whose habitation is high; You who say in your heart, 'Who will bring me down to the ground?' Though you ascend as high as the eagle, and though you set your nest among the stars, from there I will bring you down," says the Lord. "If thieves had come to you,

if robbers by night—Oh, how you will be cut off!—would they not have stolen till they had enough? If grape-gatherers had come to you, would they not have left some gleanings? Oh, how Esau shall be searched out! How his hidden treasures shall be sought after! All the men in your confederacy shall force you to the border; the men at peace with you shall deceive you and prevail against you. Those who eat your bread shall lay a trap for you. No one is aware of it. "Will I not in that day," says the LORD, "Even destroy the wise men from Edom, and understanding from the mountains of Esau? Then your mighty men, O Teman, shall be dismayed, to the end that everyone from the mountains of Esau may be cut off by slaughter." (Obadiah 1:1–9)

Now, let's return to the story of Jacob wrestling with God.

Jacob's back is up against the wall. While he was away, Esau had grown in strength. Remember, the prophetic word of Isaac was that Esau would live by the sword. While Jacob was accumulating wealth and growing his family, Esau was building an army. If there was ever a time Jacob needed God to move on his behalf, it was right now. Laban was nothing but an inconvenience in Jacob's life compared to Esau.

There are times in our lives of complete desperation. It is in those night seasons when we grab hold of God and refuse to let go, that transforming grace is released in our lives. There was a good chance Esau would have wanted to confront Jacob in hand-to-hand combat. I wonder if Jacob was praying, "LORD, make me a warrior to face Esau!" I know any of us would be praying those words in those circumstances. Yet, God's ways are not our ways. In this Christophany, the Almighty touched Jacob's hip socket and dislodged it. Imagine praying for Ninja-like skills and walking away with a bad limp! What we miss, if we're not careful, is that the Almighty changed Jacob's walk (and his paradigm). The only way he could adequately walk was to lean onto his staff (the leadership God had given him), rather than rely on his own strength. Jacob entered the wrestling event with enough stamina to wrestle with

God all night, but he left the fight utterly dependent on God alone! This transformation was so profound in Jacob's life that God changed his name to "Israel," which means "God prevails."[33] God prevailed in the wrestling with Jacob and in Jacob's situation with Esau.

In letters to the seven churches in the book of Revelation, we find this promise:

> He who has an ear, let him hear what the Spirit says to the churches. To him who overcomes I will give some of the hidden manna to eat. And I will give him a white stone, and on the stone a new name written which no one knows except him who receives it. (Revelation 2:17)

In this same letter to the church at Pergamos, we discover great persecution of God's people. We're told this is the place where the throne of Satan dwells.

> And to the angel of the church in Pergamos write, "These things says He who has the sharp two-edged sword: I know your works, and where you dwell, where Satan's throne is. And you hold fast to My name, and did not deny My faith even in the days in which Antipas was My faithful martyr, who was killed among you, where Satan dwells. (Revelation 2:12–13)

In America, we are hampered by the historical affluence of the Church. We think persecution is when someone looks at us in a mean way or lies about us. However, present-day persecution is real worldwide. Just ask our brothers and sisters in China or Muslim-controlled countries. While the luciferian elite are bringing this persecution to a new level in the Western world, it is yet to be seen how drastic it will become in the United States.

Years ago, when the Soviet Union was still a potent threat to freedom worldwide, I was serving in the military in Germany. While there,

I had the fortune of meeting with a veteran missionary who had served behind the Iron Curtain of communism in the Soviet Union. I asked this man of God what the believers were praying for regarding the Church in America. In my mind, I was thinking they might be praying God would do something like prompt more Americans to give to the missionary efforts and send more Bibles. But, to my astonishment, he replied they were praying "that enough persecution would come on the Church in America so that it would stop playing games and become the real Church!" Our conversation was very short that day.

I'm not saying persecution will need to come into our lives to trigger transformational grace. I believe that, for many, persecution can be the instrument of last resort in the toolbox of God. He prefers that all of us yield to His transformational work in our lives now. However, hubris is rampant in the American Church. Like the congregation in Laodicea, we have confused affluence with spirituality. The truth is that, spiritually, we are naked, blind, and poor. Many of the most successful ministries in America are spiritually bankrupt. We have allowed other spirits to come into our meetings, manifesting false signs and wonders that are extrabiblical. While this supernatural hype brings in crowds and large offerings, it produces no lasting spiritual fruit in the lives of believers.

To the affluent of his day, the Apostle James provides the following instructions:

> Or do you think that the Scripture says in vain, "The Spirit who dwells in us yearns jealously"? But He gives more grace. Therefore He says: **"God resists the proud, but gives grace to the humble."** Therefore submit to God. Resist the devil and he will flee from you. Draw near to God and He will draw near to you. Cleanse your hands, you sinners; and purify your hearts, you double-minded. Lament and mourn and weep! Let your laughter be turned to mourning and your joy to gloom. Humble yourselves in the sight of the Lord, and He will lift you up. (James 4:5–10, emphasis added)

As a long-time student of revival in Church history, I've learned that, historically, every true biblical revival has been preceded by the Holy Spirit pouring out grace that caused the community to move into deep repentance and to spiritually clean house. Jesus' central message during His ministry on earth was: "Repent, for the kingdom of heaven is at hand" (Matthew 4:17). That is still His message to all the earth today... including the Church!

I also discovered that before I experienced spiritual promotion, the Holy Spirit moved in my life and led me to a season of personal repentance. Yet, there are ministries today that are espousing a repentance-free gospel and a repentance-free life. But such a concept is foreign to the teachings of Scripture and disarms the Body of Christ. We need to realize repentance is not only a spiritual weapon but also a weapon of mass destruction (WMD) as far as the enemy is concerned. Years of planning and diligent efforts by the enemy to circumvent our victory can be decimated in a single moment through heartfelt repentance.

I've also discovered something else about repentance. The enemy is incapable of it. Repentance is a working of grace connected to an aspect of God (*YHVH*) that was never revealed to the angels. Therefore, he can't see it coming. It's like a sucker punch in the stomach every time a believer is cornered by the enemy and then is moved by the Holy Spirit into a season of repentance and realignment with the Kingdom.

In this critical hour in prophetic history, we must not allow false teachers and prophets to convince us to abandon this powerful weapon in our spiritual arsenal!

Empowering Grace

Now the angel who talked with me came back and wakened me, as a man who is wakened out of his sleep. And he said to me, "What do you see?" So I said, "I am looking, and there is a lampstand of solid gold with a bowl on top of it, and on the stand seven lamps with seven pipes to the seven lamps. Two olive trees are by it, one at the right of the bowl and the other at its left." So I answered and spoke to the angel who talked with me, saying, "What are these, my lord?" Then the angel who talked with me answered and said to me, "Do you not know what these are?" And I said, "No, my lord." So he answered and said to me: "This is the word of the LORD to Zerubbabel: 'Not by might nor by power, but by My Spirit,' Says the LORD of hosts. 'Who are you, O great mountain? Before Zerubbabel you shall become a plain! And he shall bring forth the capstone with shouts of "Grace, grace to it!"'" Moreover the word of the LORD came to me, saying: "The hands of Zerubbabel Have laid the foundation of this temple; His hands shall also finish it. Then you will know that the Lord of hosts has sent Me to you. For who has despised the day of small things? For these seven rejoice to see the plumb line in the hand of Zerubbabel. They are the eyes of the Lord, which scan to and fro throughout the whole earth." (Zechariah 4:1–10)

Judah had been in captivity in Babylon, but now they were returning to Jerusalem. For twenty-one years, they had attempted to rebuild the Temple on their own. For twenty-one years, all of Hell had stood in their way. From secret whisper campaigns in the ears of the Persian king to acts of economic warfare and terrorism, the enemy pulled out every trick in the book to impede their efforts. Then Almighty God began to release His prophets. First, Habakkuk came to stir the children of Israel to action. Then other prophets, like Zechariah, began to speak forth the word of the LORD. The anointing on these ancient Hebrew prophets released empowering grace into the lives of God's people. Zachariah's prophetic word targeted Zerubbabel. Almighty God was going to release a grace into the heart of Zerubbabel that would allow him to set the cornerstone of the Temple and complete it. As Zerubbabel laid the cornerstone, he was instructed to cry out "grace" twice. The first "grace" was to begin the work, and the second was to enable him to complete his divine assignment.

Grace empowers the believer. Grace enables the believer to receive salvation. Grace also empowers the believer to live free from the power of sin. Every Kingdom assignment we are given must be saturated in grace for it to be brought to fruition. Grace is an active and vital empowerment in the life of every believer.

Yet today, some in ministry use grace as an occasion to sin. God forbid! Grace does not change the nature of sin to make it more palatable to God. Instead, grace empowers the believer to overcome sin and walk in righteousness. Where sin used to abound in our lives, let it be replaced with God's grace to walk in His Kingdom.

Enduring Grace

For though I might desire to boast, I will not be a fool; for I will speak the truth. But I refrain, lest anyone should think of me above what he sees me to be or hears from me. And lest I should be exalted above measure by the abundance of the revelations, a thorn in the flesh was given to me, a messenger of Satan to buffet me, lest I be exalted above measure. Concerning this thing I pleaded with the Lord three times that it might depart from me. And He said to me, "My grace is sufficient for you, for My strength is made perfect in weakness." Therefore most gladly I will rather boast in my infirmities, that the power of Christ may rest upon me. Therefore I take pleasure in infirmities, in reproaches, in needs, in persecutions, in distresses, for Christ's sake. For when I am weak, then I am strong. (2 Corinthians 12:6–10)

Over the centuries, there has been much debate regarding the Apostle Paul's "thorn in the flesh." While some endorse the belief that the thorn is a possible physical sickness or disorder, others believe it was a relational issue. In a quick review of the book of Acts, relational seems to be the more probable nature of Paul's buffeting. Paul Barnett is a biblical scholar and the author of *The New International Commentary on the New Testament Volume of Second Corinthians*. Here is what he shares regarding the thorn in Paul's flesh:

> If, indeed, the *skolops* is relational, what—specifically—might it have been? Less likely is the suggestion that the *skolops* is the Corinthian church (or a section thereof). More plausibly, Paul's *skolops* is the rise of the Judaizing, anti-Paul movement, such as was then all too obvious in Corinth. In favor of this possibility, we note that (1) such a view would be consistent with the chronological sequence implicit in this passage—the escape from Damascus (11:32–33) *c.* a.d. 34/35, the "Paradise" experience (12:2–4) *c.* a.d. 42, and now, on this hypothesis, the rise of the anti-Pauline mission *c.* a.d. 47 (Gal 2:1, 4–5, 12–14); (2) the *skolops* as a "messenger of Satan" is matched by the false apostles who are "ministers of Satan" (11:15), false brothers who are the source of danger (see on 11:26); and (3) in the LXX, as noted above, *skolops* is used of the enemies of Israel (Num 33:55; Ezek 28:24), making the present opponents the enemies of the true Israel of God and of Paul his minister (cf. Gal 6:16).[34]

I want to point out that the Greek word *skolops* is the word Paul used for "thorn." I do enjoy Barnett's honesty in this argument regarding Paul's thorn. He continues:

> On grounds of historical analysis, however, the truth is that we do not have enough unambiguous information to do more than speculate on the nature of Paul's *skolops*. It is hard to choose between the chief options, the *physical* or the *relational*; there are weak points in both (e.g., [a] the difficulty that so robust a man as Paul evidently was (see on 11:23–33) could at the same time be physically debilitated, or [b] understanding that Paul's

"messenger of Satan" [singular] could apply to a *group* or *movement*, or [c] that Paul would say that *God* gave him something as evil as the Judaizing movement [see on 11:13–15]). Neither hypothesis is without questions, whichever one favors.

Doubtless speculations will continue to be made. Pastorally, however, it may be to our advantage not to know. The very openness of the identification allows wide possibilities of personal application to a broad range of personal suffering, which precise identification might limit.[35]

While biblical scholars share in their honesty that we cannot draw an exact identification from the text, believers all over the Internet slug it out that their position is correct. Barnett may be right. We should allow for a broad range of personal applications regarding the grace of God. (And may God's grace also take hold of believers' debates on the Internet.)

The lesson to be learned from Paul's answer that God's grace is enough is reassuring for all believers of every generation. What the grace of God will not deliver us from will give us the endurance to walk through. Grace is so much more than we could have ever imagined!

Growing in Grace and the Covenants of the Bible

Over the years, I noticed a corresponding pattern of spiritual growth found in the types of covenants, the cups used in Passover, and the four types of baptism (Mikveh) revealed in the Word of God. Nearly two decades ago, I was teaching these concepts at a seminar in Minnesota. At the lunch break, a young man came up to me and handed me a book, the authors of which had already written on the subject in more detail than I was providing in the seminar. The title of the book is *Lost in Translation—Volume 1: Rediscovering the Hebrew Roots of Our Faith* and it's written by John Klein and Adam Spears. I've made a chart from this book that reveals the correlation between the types of covenants, cups of Passover, and baptisms, and how they represent growing in grace.

Covenants and Mikvehs[36]

Covenant	Cups	Mikveh
Blood	Servant	Repentance
Salt	Friendship	Dedication
Sandal	Inheritance	Ministry
Marriage	Marriage	Marriage

This chart shows the growth in grace believers are supposed to experience in their walk with God.

- ❖ The blood covenant is a covenant to servanthood and is entered through repentance.
- ❖ The salt covenant is a covenant of friendship and is entered through dedication.
- ❖ The sandal covenant is a covenant of inheritance and is entered as a part of ministry.
- ❖ The final stage is represented by marriage in all three categories. Of course, every believer's goal is to celebrate the Marriage Supper of the Lamb.

Careful examination of this chart will reveal a progressive theme of growing intimacy with God. Biblically, the ultimate level of intimacy is represented in the marriage covenant. This also presents a spiritual paradox we discovered in the story of Jacob and empowering grace: God is made strong in our weakness. Jacob faced an impossible situation when he had to come face to face with Esau. Physical strength was not going to win the day for Jacob. This patriarch of the faith discovered the only way to win in this situation was to be utterly dependent upon Almighty God. In that moment, the LORD went before him and touched the heart of Esau.

We read a powerful truth in the book of Proverbs:

When a man's ways please the LORD, he makes even his enemies to be at peace with him. (Proverbs 16:7)

The task of the true Kingdom warrior is twofold:

1. To be skillful in the art and mindset of spiritual warfare.
2. To become an expert at leaning into God in every situation.

Prayer

Father, I come to you humbly with a heart's desire to know you more fully and to mature in every aspect of your grace. I do not desire to lean upon my understanding or strength, but to lean more fully into your arms in every life situation. Let me never wrestle away from you, but fight to get closer to you with each passing day. Only when I am entirely dependent upon you will I discover what it is to become a Kingdom warrior fighting to fulfill my King's desires in the earth, in Jesus' name.

Review Questions

1. In 1 Peter 5:10, the Apostle Peter speaks of the "God of all grace." According to the *New Testament and Other Early Christian Literature (BDAG)*, what does the Greek word for "all" mean?

2. How many aspects of grace, according to the author, are revealed in the Word of God? What are they?

3. In the Creation story, the Creator is referred to as *Elohim* in the Hebrew text. When God created humans, what new aspect of Himself did He reveal through the name *YHVH-Elohim*?

4. According to the apostles, who is the Creator?

5. Through the power of the Holy Spirit, what is our first act of spiritual authority?

6. Even when grace is extended by God to those who have sinned, can there still be consequences for their actions?

7. In the story of Jacob wrestling with God all night, what lesson can we learn about spiritual warfare?

8. In reference to repentance, what type of spiritual weapon is it?

THE BINARY NATURE OF
THE SPIRIT REALM

> I call heaven and earth as witnesses today against you, that I have
> set before you life and death, blessing and cursing; therefore choose
> life, that both you and your descendants may live; that you may
> love the LORD your God, that you may obey His voice, and that
> you may cling to Him, for He is your life and the length of your
> days; and that you may dwell in the land which the LORD swore to
> your fathers, to Abraham, Isaac, and Jacob, to give them.
>
> DEUTERONOMY 30:19–20

At the point we find the nation of Israel in Deuteronomy 30, they fully understood the ways of Egypt. The people of God had spent four hundred years there, both enjoying prosperity and enduring the harsh realities of slavery. No one had to teach them what the mystery religions were or how to worship the gods of Egypt. Every Israelite was an expert. If we examine the story of Aaron creating the golden calf in Moses' absence, we will not find him looking at reference books on Egypt regarding its construction. Nor did the children of Israel need to be instructed on what to do in the worship of the golden calf. Every one of them knew. After centuries of captivity under the yoke of Egypt, the

Israelites knew about the sexual debauchery involved in their pagan worship. In Exodus 32:6, we read that, during the blasphemous manufactured feast, the children of Israel "rose up to play." Be assured that their play was adult in nature and undoubtedly XXX-rated. Their paganized, debauchery-filled pseudo-worship caused the Almighty to send Moses down from the mountain, and he brought judgment with him.

In their present state, Israel did not know how to serve this God who had delivered them from Egyptian bondage. These formerly enslaved people didn't know what the God of Abraham, Isaac, and Jacob considered to be sin or righteous acts in His eyes. The cure for the infection of Egypt upon their souls was the Torah of God. The same can be said of the Church today. Even after we are saved (i.e., delivered from the Pharaoh of this world), no one needs to teach us how to sin. Sin comes naturally to the old nature. However, we need to have our minds renewed by the Word of God so we might learn how to serve and walk with God. This God of the Hebrews has adopted us and grafted us into His Kingdom. The Kingdom of God is unique and unlike any other kingdom on the planet. The Apostle Paul reminds us of this in Romans 12:1–2:

> I beseech you therefore, brethren, by the mercies of God, that you present your bodies a living sacrifice, holy, acceptable to God, which is your reasonable service. And do not be conformed to this world, but be transformed by the renewing of your mind, that you may prove what *is* that good and acceptable and perfect will of God. (Romans 12:1–2)

When Paul penned these anointed words, the New Testament did not exist. It would not exist for about another three hundred years. (The New Testament was canonized in AD 367) What did exist were the books of Genesis through Malachi: the books that comprise the First Testament (or Old Testament). I have been amazed over the years at how many ministers glaze over one statement in the ruling of the apostolic council regarding Gentiles coming into the faith. Here is that statement:

For Moses has had throughout many generations those who preach him in every city, being read in the synagogues every Sabbath. (Acts 15:21)

At that time in Church history, the Gentiles coming into the faith were God-fearers. This may be an unfamiliar term to the twenty-first-century Church, but it had a specific meaning to the first-century one. God-fearers were Gentiles who walked in the commandments of God, kept the feasts of the LORD, ate biblically clean foods (the reason it was not brought up before the council), and had done everything except become physically Jewish through circumcision. Some may have come to faith years before and others more recently (just like we all do in life today). The apostles came to realize a truth that was shown to the Apostle Paul: There is a greater circumcision—the circumcision of the heart, which was prophesied by the ancient prophets of Israel. Many biblical scholars believe this revelation was given to Paul when he was taken up to the Third Heaven and personally taught by the LORD (2 Corinthians 12:2). With these new believers in Messiah, the First Testament would serve the same purpose as it did for the Israelites coming out of Egypt. The Hebrew Scriptures would teach them how to walk with the God who had just delivered them. The God of the Bible is completely different from the gods of the mystery religions. How we show our love for God is diametrically opposed to how pagans serve their gods.

Unfortunately, thanks to a heretic named Marcion in the second century, and later through a Catholic theologian named Augustine (who picked up some of Marcion's teachings), we have been programmed with innate jaundice for the instruction of God.

The Hebrew word *Torah* means "to hit the mark." It depicts a father teaching his son how to shoot an arrow. The young child's arrow falls short of the target, so the father gently leans over and says, "Son, aim a little higher next time." *Moody's Theological Workbook of the Old Testament* notes:

The word *târâ* means basically "teaching" whether it is the wise man instructing his son or God instructing Israel. The wise give insight into all aspects of life so that the young may know how to conduct themselves and to live a long, blessed life (Proverbs 3:1f.). So too God, motivated by love, reveals to man basic insight into how to live with each other and how to approach God. Through the law God shows his interest in all aspects of man's life which is to be lived under his direction and care. Law of God stands parallel to word of the Lord to signify that law is the revelation of God's will (e.g. Isaiah 1:10). In this capacity it becomes the nation's wisdom and understanding so that others will marvel at the quality of Israel's distinctive lifestyle (Deut. 4:6). Thus, there is a very similar understanding of the role of teaching with its results in the wisdom school, in the priestly instruction, and the role of the law with its results for all the people of the covenant.[37]

Dr. Ron Moseley shares the historical story of Marcion in his book, *Yeshua: The Real Jesus and the Early Church.*

The teaching that the Law of God was superseded by, or in opposition to, the grace of God did not originate with Paul, but with a heretical sect called the Marcions and their interpretation of Paul's writings.

Marcion, the Source of Much Confusion Concerning the Law

Marcion, who lived during the second century AD, rejected the Old Testament completely. Having been greatly influenced by the Gnostics, he taught a demiurgic notion that the God of the Old Testament was cruel and totally different from the God revealed in the New Testament. He was so consumed with the belief that Paul's message of God's grace opposed God's Law that he kept only an edited portion of Paul's writings that agreed with his theology. Marcion's view was so contrary to God's Word that Polycarp, a student of John, called him "the firstborn of Satan."

Marcion went to Rome sometime around AD 139 and made a generous gift to the Church. After examining his views, the congregation gave back his money and excommunicated him. Marcion subsequently founded his own church, which merged Gnosticism with orthodox Christianity, creating a theology that was sharply dualistic, violently antagonistic toward Judaism, strictly ascetic and celibate, and that wielded a wide and destructive influence throughout Christendom. Unfortunately, some modern Christians have unknowingly endorsed his ideas.

Later, the Roman Catholic monk Augustine championed Marcion's ideas about grace opposing God's Law and made them a significant part of his theology.[38]

It should be noted that, after his rejection by the Church in Rome, Marcion taught that Jesus was a completely different God than the Old Testament one, that Jesus had conquered God and had done away with His horrid Law.

It's All in the Translation

As I have already explained, the word for "law" in Hebrew is *torah,* and it means "the loving instruction of the Father." However, the first problem we run into is that the Greek language did not have a word to express this truth. So, another word was substituted. The writers of the New Testament (and the Septuagint) used the Greek word *nomos,* which means "anything established, anything received by usage, a custom, a law, a command, of any law whatsoever, and a law or rule producing a state approved of God."[39] In the Greek culture, the concept of law had nothing to do with love. To the Greeks, the law was about democracy and the people's will. The idea of the law being the loving instruction of the heavenly Father was lost in translation. But it doesn't stop there. The Catholic Church translated the Bible into Latin. The Latin word for "law" is *lex*, which means, "law, compact, ordinance, contract, stipulation, regulation, code, decree, and statute."[40] The concept of law shifted first from loving instruction to no love just law, and finally through Latin, the concept of the harshness of Roman law. Roman law was exact, strict, overbearing, and without mercy (think "crucifixion of any who opposed Roman rule and law"). Today, much of the Church draws its attitude regarding the Law of God from Latin rather than the original Hebrew (as well as Catholic theology, which replaced God's Law with the traditions of Christendom[41]).

With the 613 commandments in the Torah, God established a nation and created civil law, moral law, and regulations regarding the priesthood. This is mind-boggling! Just 613 laws or commandments to run an entire country. Compare this to the millions of laws and regulations on the books in America. The Torah was, in many ways, a legislative miracle. Do not confuse the Torah with the Talmud. Starting in the Second Temple period, the rabbis began adding their own regulations to what God had given Moses. To add weight to their man-made rules, they called these regulations "Oral Torah." Here is what Jesus had to say about their additions to the writings of Moses:

> ...making the word of God of no effect through your tradition
> which you have handed down. And many such things you do.
> (Mark 7:13)

This gravitation toward oral law inevitably replaced the Law of God. What became a subtle rejection of Moses finally became a complete replacement. The genesis of this transition existed in the time of Jesus, and He knew where it was heading. Jesus connected this rejection of Moses with His rejection as Messiah.

Do not think that I shall accuse you to the Father; there is one who accuses you—Moses, in whom you trust. For if you believed Moses, you would believe Me; for he wrote about Me. But if you do not believe his writings, how will you believe My words? (John 5:45–47)

Those who have read my previous books understand that my interest in the Torah is regarding the moral law. For the Gentile New Testament believer (if you will), Paul never taught the Gentiles to be culturally Jewish. He did, however, teach them the moral requirements of the Law of God. Whatever God has declared to be a sinful act will always be a sinful act. The cross did not change sin; it freed the believer from the power of sin.

It was Maimonides[42] who first codified the Law in his work, the *Mishneh Torah*. He compiled what was considered his magnum opus (his most significant work) between AD 1170 and AD 1180.[43] While this work's primary focus was on the oral law, he did break down the Law of Moses into several categories:

- ✢ Ceremonial law (The priesthood and religious rites)
- ✢ Civil law (Law that governed Israel)
- ✢ Moral law (the moral requirements of the God of Israel)

While I agree with his categorization for the most part, I do recognize there can be an overlapping of the civil and moral law and ceremonial and moral law in rare instances. For the early Church, including the Gentile believers, understanding the moral requirements of God was essential to walking with Messiah. The Apostle John, in one of the last books written in the Second (or New) Testament, reminds us:

Whoever commits sin also commits lawlessness, and sin is lawlessness. (1 John 3:4)

The Greek word used for "lawlessness" in the NKJV is *anomia* (*an-om-ee'-ah*), which means "the condition of without law; because ignorant of it; because of violating it; contempt and violation of law, iniquity, wickedness."[44] This is why the KJV translates this word as "law." Biblically, lawlessness is the state of rejecting the Law of God.

Why is all of this so important for the believer today?

> I call heaven and earth as witnesses today against you, that I have set before you life and death, blessing and cursing; therefore choose life, that both you and your descendants may live; that you may love the LORD your God, that you may obey His voice, and that you may cling to Him, for He is your life and the length of your days; and that you may dwell in the land which the LORD swore to your fathers, to Abraham, Isaac, and Jacob, to give them. (Deuteronomy 30:19–20)

Deuteronomy 30 was written after the wandering in the wilderness was ending. An unfaithful generation that rejected God's instruction to cross over the Jordan had passed away (except for Joshua and Caleb). This new generation had been taught the ways of God from birth. Therefore, they understood the difference between the ways of God and the ways of the pagan nations around them. There were two doors open to them. Sin opens the door to Hell, while living according to God's ways opens the door to Heaven. In the spirit realm, everything is binary. By using the term "binary," I'm referring to computer programming. In binary code, the ones and zeroes are either opening or closing switches in the computer's processing core. What we think, say, and do can either close or open doors to Heaven and Hell. During the process of sanctification in our lives, the blessings begin to flow when we have more doors open to Heaven than to Hell. Unfortunately, because of the lack of proper discipleship in the modern Church, we have ended up with a form of godliness that has no power (2 Timothy 3:5). To be honest, most believers today have more doors open in their lives to the enemy than to Heaven. In their desperation for some kind of relief from the constant bombardment from the enemy, they run from one meeting to another seeking someone with enough anointing to provide relief (even if it is temporary). Too many of these believers inevitably run into the arms of false teachers who promise quick fixes that require no significant work or life change on their part (other than the skill to send in ever-increasing offerings).

There is hard work involved in the dynamic transformation the Apostle Paul refers to in Romans 12:1–2. Let's look at those verses:

> I beseech you therefore, brethren, by the mercies of God, that you present your bodies a living sacrifice, holy, acceptable to God, which is your reasonable service. And do not be conformed to this world, but be transformed by the renewing of your mind, that you may prove what is that good and acceptable and perfect will of God. (Romans 12:1–2)

The Greek word Paul uses for "prove" is *dokimazo* (*dok-im-ad'-zo*), which means "to test, examine, prove, scrutinize (to see whether a thing is genuine or not), as metals; to recognize as genuine after examination, to approve, deem worthy."[45]

Douglas J. Moo is a respected biblical scholar and the professor of biblical studies at Wheaton College Graduate School. In his volume on Romans for the *New International Commentary of the New Testament*, he makes this observation of Romans 12:2:

> "The renewing of your mind" is the means by which this transformation takes place. "Mind" translates a word that Paul uses especially to connote a person's "practical reason," or "moral consciousness." Christians are to adjust their way of thinking about everything in accordance with the "newness" of their life in the Spirit (cf. 7:6). This "re-programming" of the mind does not take place overnight but is a lifelong process by which our way

of thinking is to resemble more and more the way God wants us
to think. In Rom. 1:28 Paul has pointed out that people's rejection
of God has resulted in God's giving them over to a "worthless"
mind: one that is "unqualified" *(adokimos)* in assessing the truth
about God and the world he has made. Now, Paul asserts, the purpose of our being transformed by the renewing of the mind is that
this state might be reversed; that we might be able to "approve"
(dokimazō) the will of God. "Approving" the will of God means
to understand and agree with what God wants of us with a view to
putting it into practice. That Paul means here by "the will of God"
his moral direction is clear from the way Paul describes it: this will
is that which is "good," "acceptable [to God]," and "perfect."[46]

Do the lives of believers today prove what is the good, acceptable,
and perfect will of God? Can they even discern God's will?

While "work" seems to be a four-letter word to the modern Church,
the Apostle Paul was never afraid to use it. Read his counsel in Philippians 2:

> Therefore, my beloved, as you have always obeyed, not as in
> my presence only, but now much more in my absence, work
> out your own salvation with fear and trembling; for it is God
> who works in you both to will and to do for His good pleasure.
> (Philippians 2:12–13)

This reprogramming of our minds to God's moral code is hard work
and a vital part of spiritual transformation. We cannot think like a slave
of the kingdom of darkness and act like a citizen of the Kingdom of God
at the same time. They are two different kingdoms with diametrically
opposed cultures and laws. Did you know that Hell has a law, or *torah*?
In the book of Romans, Paul speaks of "another law" that was connected
to his carnal nature:

Therefore the law is holy, and the commandment holy and just and good. Has then what is good become death to me? Certainly not! But sin, that it might appear sin, was producing death in me through what is good, so that sin through the commandment might become exceedingly sinful. For we know that the law is spiritual, but I am carnal, sold under sin. For what I am doing, I do not understand. For what I will to do, that I do not practice; but what I hate, that I do. If, then, I do what I will not to do, I agree with the law that it is good. But now, it is no longer I who do it, but sin that dwells in me. For I know that in me (that is, in my flesh) nothing good dwells; for to will is present with me, but how to perform what is good I do not find. For the good that I will to do, I do not do; but the evil I will not to do, that I practice. Now if I do what I will not to do, it is no longer I who do it, but sin that dwells in me. I find then a law, that evil is present with me, the one who wills to do good. For I delight in the law of God according to the inward man. But I see another law in my members, warring against the law of my mind, and bringing me into captivity to the law of sin which is in my members. (Romans 7:12–23)

In this powerful rabbinical argument that the Apostle Paul puts forth in the book of Romans, he describes a great internal conflict. As a child, Paul had been taught the Torah. The apostle was at least a second-generation Pharisee (Acts 23:6), and, according to his testimony, well after he came to faith, he lived as a strict Pharisee (Acts 26:5). Yet before he came to faith in Messiah, he reveals, in his sin nature, another law had existed that warred against his knowledge of the Word and requirements of God. Later in this theological argument, this seasoned rabbi reveals that it had been Messiah who set him free from the old person filled with death. Paul declares:

I thank God—through Jesus Christ our Lord! So then, with the mind I myself serve the law of God, but with the flesh the law of sin. (Romans 7:25)

Remember there are two *torahs*. With that in mind, let's now read the first verses in the next chapter of Romans, chapter 8 (remember, chapters and verses are artificial separations created by scholars):

There is therefore now no condemnation to those who are in Christ Jesus, who do not walk according to the flesh, but according to the Spirit. For the law of the Spirit of life in Christ Jesus has made me free from the law of sin and death. For what the law could not do in that it was weak through the flesh, God did by sending His own Son in the likeness of sinful flesh, on account of sin: He condemned sin in the flesh, that the righteous requirement of the law might be fulfilled in us who do not walk according to the flesh but according to the Spirit. For those who live according to the flesh set their minds on the things of the flesh, but those who live according to the Spirit, the things of the Spirit. For to be carnally minded is death, but to be spiritually minded is life and peace. (Romans 8:1–6)

We must understand what Paul has already established in chapter 7 to keep track of what he is referring to in chapter 8. There are two laws: one from Heaven and one from Hell. Walking in the flesh is walking in the *torah*, or law, of Hell. He reveals that the only way the Law of God can properly be lived is through Messiah by the power of the Holy Spirit. In verse 4, Paul reveals that through Messiah the Law is fulfilled in the life of the believer. The Greek word Paul uses for "fulfilled" is the exact same word Jesus used in Matthew 5:17–19:

Do not think that I came to destroy the Law or the Prophets. I did not come to destroy but to fulfill. For assuredly, I say to you, till heaven and earth pass away, one jot or one tittle will by no means pass from the law till all is fulfilled. Whoever therefore breaks one of the least of these commandments, and teaches men so, shall be called least in the kingdom of heaven; but whoever does and teaches them, he shall be called great in the kingdom of heaven.

The Greek word both Jesus and Paul used is *pleroo* (*play-ro'-o*). Here's what it means: "to make full, to fill up, i.e. to fill to the full; to cause to abound, to furnish or supply liberally; I abound, I am liberally supplied; to render full, i.e. to complete."[47] (Although the full definition is much longer, no interpretation of this word would include the concept of a contract being fulfilled and done away with). By the Apostle Paul using the same terminology Jesus used in the famous Sermon on the Mount, he is giving testimony to the truthfulness of Messiah's promise! The Law of God can only find its full expression in the life of a believer walking in the Spirit!

This interpretation, keeping in line with the historical and contextual settings, flies in the face of what is being preached in many pulpits today. I was taught that the "law of sin and death" was the Torah. Yet, this nebulous "law of the Spirit of life in Christ Jesus" is left undefined and relegated to the mysterious moving and empowerment of the Holy Spirit. But, according to Paul, nothing could be farther from the truth.

Jeremiah foresaw the revelation Paul declares in the book of Romans:

Behold, the days are coming, says the LORD, when I will make a new covenant with the house of Israel and with the house of Judah—not according to the covenant that I made with their fathers in the day that I took them by the hand to lead them out of the land of Egypt, My covenant which they broke, though I was a husband to them, says the LORD. But this is the covenant that I will make with the house of Israel after those days, says the Lord: I will put My law in their minds, and write it on their hearts; and I will be their God, and they shall be My people. (Jeremiah 31:31–33)

This one prophetic word from the prophet Jeremiah is where the concepts of the New Covenant and New Testament are drawn from theologically. This New Covenant is transformational. God, Himself, will write His commandments (Law) upon the hearts and establish them within the minds of those who enter that covenant. Supernaturally walking in God's ways (following His commandments) is an essential part of the new birth in Christ! Paul uses this concept to metaphorically slap the Pharisees upside the head; that's what caused the problems in Acts 15. Consider his argument about why these saved Gentiles should be accepted in the Jewish community.

For there is no partiality with God. For as many as have sinned without law will also perish without law, and as many as have sinned in the law will be judged by the law (for not the hearers of the law are just in the sight of God, but the doers of the law will be justified; for when Gentiles, who do not have the law, by nature do the things in the law, these, although not having the law, are a law to themselves, who show the work of the law written in their hearts, their conscience also bearing witness, and between themselves their thoughts accusing or else excusing them) in the day when God will judge the secrets of men by Jesus Christ, according to my gospel. (Romans 2:11–16)

Paul told the Pharisees of his day, "You teach the Law but cannot keep it." These Gentiles were not raised being taught the Law, but were keeping it because faith in Messiah was written it in their hearts. Every rabbi who read this statement knew well that Paul was referring to Jeremiah 31! A New Covenant through Messiah had been established, and those unlearned Gentiles were living what the rabbis could not. WOW!

Paul continues to connect the "fulfilling" (to fill full of meaning and to abound) of the Law through faith in Messiah in Romans 13:8–10.

> Owe no one anything except to love one another, for he who loves another has fulfilled the law. For the commandments, "You shall not commit adultery," "You shall not murder," "You shall not steal," "You shall not bear false witness," "You shall not covet," and if there is any other commandment, are all summed up in this saying, namely, "You shall love your neighbor as yourself." Love does no harm to a neighbor; therefore love is the fulfillment of the law.

In Romans 13:8, Paul uses the same Greek word he uses in Romans 8:4: *pleroo*. However, in his statement in verse 10 of Romans 13, he uses the Greek word *pleroma* (*play'-ro-mah*) for "fulfillment." *Pleroma* can be defined as follows:

> That which is (has been) filled; a ship inasmuch as it is filled (i.e., manned) with sailors, rowers, and soldiers; in the NT, the body of believers, as that which is filled with the presence, power, agency, riches of God and of Christ; that which fills or with which a thing is filled; of those things which a ship is filled, freight and merchandise, sailors, oarsmen, soldiers; completeness or fullness of time; fullness, abundance; a fulfilling, keeping.[48]

This word paints a powerful picture. The Law is the ship. It can sit in the harbor empty and useless. However, the love of God (and love for God) is released in the hearts of believers by the Holy Spirit (Romans 5:5), causing the ship (Law) to be fully manned and filled with abundance. In the ancient world, communities would rejoice when merchant ships came into port. The local merchants' storerooms would be replenished. Hard-to-find items would be restocked on store shelves. The ships were the life's blood of the community. It is the same today.

When believers walk out the commandments of God because of their love for God and one another, it causes the Christian community to move in the abundance of Heaven. The very purpose of the ways of God is being established, and its intent is manifested among God's people.

As the Gentiles were coming to faith in Messiah and abandoning the paganism within their cultures to replace it with the ways of the Kingdom, they were systematically closing the doors to the enemy their previous lifestyles had opened. Remember, in the days of the Apostle Paul, for a Gentile to come to the faith required a complete overhaul of their beliefs, lifestyles, and participation in the culture around them. There was a real cost to following Jesus for these first-century Gentile believers. They would be ostracized and persecuted by friends, family, and their communities.

Biblically, walking in the Spirit is walking in the ways of God by the power of the Holy Spirit, and walking in the flesh is walking in the ways of Hell by demonic power. Our thoughts, words, or actions (whether by the Holy Spirit or demonic power) open and close doors in the spirit realm. These doors have a profound influence on our lives.

In the next chapter, we will look at a biblical example of an open door Israel created through rebellion toward God, how Satan is a legalist, and how to deal with generational tendencies and curses.

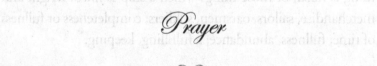

Prayer

Father, my heart desires to reject this world's ways and learn the ways of the Kingdom. I declare this day an open-door invitation to your Spirit to convict my heart of anything that needs to change to align me more fully with your Kingdom. Provide a fresh anointing to learn and walk in your Word in every area of my life. In Jesus' name.

Review Questions

1. How is Romans 12:1–2 crucial for walking in the Kingdom?
2. What important declaration regarding the ruling of the Gentiles by the Jerusalem council in Acts 15 is overlooked today?
3. Biblically, what does the word "Torah" mean?
4. How is the concept of "law" different in the Hebrew, Greek, and Roman cultures?
5. According to Jeremiah 31:31, how is the Law of God connected to the new birth?
6. What category of biblical law should apply to Gentile believers?
8. In Romans 7, does Paul reveal that there are two laws?
7. In Romans 13, what does Paul reveal about the Law of God when believers are truly walking in love?

SATAN THE LEGALIST AND CLOSING GENERATIONAL DOORS

So all the congregation lifted up their voices and cried, and the people wept that night. And all the children of Israel complained against Moses and Aaron, and the whole congregation said to them, "If only we had died in the land of Egypt! Or if only we had died in this wilderness! Why has the LORD brought us to this land to fall by the sword, that our wives and children should become victims? Would it not be better for us to return to Egypt?" So they said to one another, "Let us select a leader and return to Egypt." Then Moses and Aaron fell on their faces before all the assembly of the congregation of the children of Israel.

NUMBERS 14:1–5

The power of God had freed Israel from Egyptian slavery. Not a single man or woman had to lift a sword to gain this freedom. God had sent a redeemer into their midst to set them free. This redeemer's name was Moses. God's people walked out of Egypt with payment for their years of slavery (Exodus 12:36), had their health restored (Psalm 105:37), saw Pharaoh's army destroyed in the Red Sea (Exodus 14), and met with Almighty God at Mount Sinai with a display of power that even frightened Moses (Hebrew 12:21). When it came time for the people of God to cross over the Jordan and to take the land, they did the unthinkable. With the news of the giants living in the land, the people of God rebelled against the leadership of God as a nation and even made false accusations against the Almighty. We find this story in Numbers 14:

> So all the congregation lifted up their voices and cried, and the people wept that night. And all the children of Israel complained against Moses and Aaron, and the whole congregation said to them, "If only we had died in the land of Egypt! Or if only we had died in this wilderness! Why has the LORD brought us to this land to fall by the sword, that our wives and children should become victims? Would it not be better for us to return to Egypt?" So they said to one another, "Let us select a leader and return to Egypt." Then Moses and Aaron fell on their faces before all the assembly of the congregation of the children of Israel. But Joshua the son of Nun and Caleb the son of Jephunneh, who were among those who had spied out the land, tore their clothes; and they spoke to all the congregation of the children of Israel, saying: "The land we passed through to spy out is an exceedingly good land. If the LORD delights in us, then He will bring us into this land and give it to us, 'a land which flows with milk and honey" Only do not rebel against the LORD, nor fear the people of the land, for they are our bread; their protection has departed from them, and the LORD is with us. Do not fear them." And all the congregation said to stone them with stones. Now the glory of the LORD appeared in the tabernacle of meeting before all the children of Israel. Then the LORD said to Moses: "How long will these people reject Me? And how long will they not believe Me, with all the signs which I have performed among them? I will strike them with the pestilence and disinherit them, and I will make of you a nation greater and mightier than they." (Numbers 14:1–12)

God had delivered them, loved them, supplied their every need, and even married the nation of Israel (and eventually divorced Israel for adultery; see Jeremiah 3:8 and Hosea 1:6, 9). Yet, when it came time for them to participate actively in the promises of God, they moved in rebellion. Then carnal self-justification kicked in, and they made false accusations against God. This event so angered Almighty God that He was ready to completely wipe out all of Israel and start again with Moses. At this news, Moses stood in the gap for Israel and pleaded their case before God:

> And Moses said to the LORD: "Then the Egyptians will hear it, for by Your might You brought these people up from among them, and they will tell it to the inhabitants of this land. They have heard that You, LORD, are among these people; that You, LORD, are seen face to face and Your cloud stands above them, and You go before them in a pillar of cloud by day and in a pillar of fire by night. Now if You kill these people as one man, then the nations which have heard of Your fame will speak, saying, 'Because the LORD was not able to bring this people to the land which He swore to give them, therefore He killed them in the wilderness.' And now, I pray, let the power of my LORD be great, just as You have spoken, saying, 'The LORD is longsuffering and abundant in mercy, forgiving iniquity and transgression; but He by no means clears the guilty, visiting the iniquity of the fathers on the children to the third and fourth generation.' Pardon the iniquity of this people, I pray, according to the greatness of Your mercy, just as You have forgiven this people, from Egypt even until now." Then the LORD said: "I have pardoned, according to your word; but truly, as I live, all the earth shall be filled with the glory of the LORD." (Numbers 14:13–21)

Through Moses' intercessory ministry, God pardoned His people's rebellion. But the story doesn't stop there. Both Jewish and Christian historians have noted that Israel as a nation has never repented of the actions it took that day. There was more ahead of them than just being sentenced to wandering in the wilderness until that generation passed away. Their action that day opened a spiritual doorway for the enemy.

When we examine the history of Israel, we discover that the Temple was destroyed twice—on the exact same day, centuries apart. This date is marked on the Jewish calendar each year as *Tisha B'Av*. Many researchers have traced this date back to the time of Moses, when the children of Israel rebelled against God and refused to cross over the Jordan into the Promised Land. There are also other events in Israel's history that occurred on the exact same day of the year. An article from *One for Israel* notes the following also happened on that day in history:

✢ Tradition holds that the Bar Kokhba revolt was crushed on 9th Av in 132 A.D., and that the Romans killed 100,000 Jews.

✢ The following year on 9th Av, the Romans plowed the site of the temple area, putting salt there so nothing could grow on it.

✢ The First Crusade officially commenced on Av 9, 4856 according to the Jewish calendar (August 15, 1096 in the Gregorian calendar), killing 10,000 Jews in its first month and destroying Jewish communities in France and the Rhineland.

✢ Jews were expelled from England on Av 9, 5050 (July 25, 1290).

✢ Jews were expelled from Spain on Av 8-9, 5252 (July 31, 1492).

✢ On the eve of Tisha B'Av 5702 (July 23, 1942), the mass deportation began of Jews from the Warsaw Ghetto, en route to Treblinka.[49]

Israel's unified act of rebellion against the leadership of Almighty God opened a door that still seems to remain open.

On a personal level, actions taken by us (and past relatives), can open doors that can transcend generations. Some are manifested as generational tendencies, such as anger, self-sabotage, adultery, etc. Others are manifested as generational curses. Generational curses are usually not activated by the kingdom of darkness unless someone breaks free from their grip and tries to serve God.

As we dive into the subject of generational curses, I want to start with the Decalogue (Ten Commandments).

I am the LORD your God who brought you out of the land of Egypt, out of the house of bondage. You shall have no other gods before Me. You shall not make for yourself a carved image—any likeness of anything that is in heaven above, or that is in the earth beneath, or that is in the water under the earth; you shall not bow down to them nor serve them. For I, the LORD your God, am a jealous God, visiting the iniquity of the fathers upon the children to the third and fourth generations of those who hate Me, but showing mercy to thousands, to those who love Me and keep My commandments. You shall not take the name of the LORD your God in vain, for the LORD will not hold him guiltless who takes His name in vain. Observe the Sabbath day, to keep it holy, as the LORD your God commanded you. Six days you shall labor and do all your work, but the seventh day is the Sabbath of the LORD your God. In it you shall do no work: you, nor your son, nor your daughter, nor your male servant, nor your female servant, nor your ox, nor your donkey, nor any of your cattle, nor your stranger who is within your gates, that your male servant and your female servant may rest as well as you. And remember that you were a slave in the land of Egypt, and the LORD your God brought you out from there by a mighty hand and by an outstretched arm; therefore the LORD your God commanded you to keep the Sabbath day. Honor your father and your mother, as the LORD your God has commanded you, that your days may be long, and that it may be well with you in the land which the LORD your God is giving you. You shall not murder. You shall not commit adultery. You shall not steal. You shall not bear false witness against your neighbor. You shall not covet your neighbor's wife; and you shall not desire your neighbor's house, his field, his male servant, his female servant, his ox, his donkey, or anything that is your neighbor's. (Deuteronomy 5:6–21)

As we read through the Ten Commandments, God starts out the Decalogue remembering the episode with the golden calf. Here is a loose translation from the original Hebrew:

I am the only God that brought you out of the land of Egypt.
Do not worship other gods and stick them in my face.

If God was dwelling in the midst of His people, He was right there while they violated their covenant with Him. From a biblical point of view, to incorporate pagan practices into one's life while walking with Almighty God is spiritual adultery. Spiritual adultery can be defined in the following way:

Spiritual adultery is unfaithfulness to God. It is having an undue fondness for the things of the world. Spiritual adultery is analogous to the unfaithfulness of one's spouse: "'But like a woman faithless to her lover, even so have you been faithless to me, O house of Israel,' says the Lord." (Jeremiah 3:20; see also Isaiah 1:21; 57:8; Ezekiel 16:30.

The Bible tells us people who choose to be friends with the world are "adulterous people" having "enmity against God" (James 4:4–5). The "world" here is the system of evil under Satan's control (John 12:31; Ephesians 2:2; 1 John 5:19). The world system, with its contrived and deceitful scheme of phony values, worthless pursuits, and unnatural affections, is designed to lure us away from a pure relationship with God. Spiritual adultery, then, is the forsaking of God's love and the embracing of the world's values and desires (Romans 8:7–8; 2 Timothy 4:10; 1 John 2:15–17).

Spiritual adultery includes any form of idolatry. In the Old Testament, the children of Israel tried to mix the worship of other gods such as Baal with that of God (Judges 3:7; 1 Kings 16:31–33; Jeremiah 19:5). In doing so, Israel became like an adulterous wife who wanted both a husband and another lover (Jeremiah 9:2; Ezekiel 6:9; 16:32). In the New Testament, James defines spiritual adultery as claiming to love God while cultivating friendship with the world (James 4:4–5). People who commit spiritual adultery are those who profess to be a Christian yet find their real love and pleasure in the things Satan offers.[50]

Imagine how horrific it would be for a wife to call in another lover and commit adultery with the husband sitting in the room. Spiritually, this is what happens (from God's point of view) when we engage in pagan practices. This act is at the very top of God's list of things never to do! He equates such acts as hatred for Him (and what good and honorable husband wouldn't?). The paganization of God's people is a truly heinous act. It was so severe that God would judge the families involved up to four generations. Heaven itself would move against them for the depths of the hurt they brought to the heart of God. We say that God is love. Yet we have reduced that love to some mushy, watered-down version that would accept anything the world offers us that might appease our flesh. God's love runs deeper than we can ever imagine, and so do His emotions. So many in this world have taken Jesus' sacrifice on the cross for granted. They have spent two millennia rejecting the greatest expression of love Heaven could ever afford. Is it any wonder that, after they have embraced the son of perdition, who has done nothing for them (but has promised them everything the flesh could ever desire), Jesus would return in great wrath? The modern Church must regain a healthy reverence for Almighty God. The fear of the LORD is the beginning of wisdom

(Psalm 111:10). This judgment of God, because of the sins of the
fathers, gained an ancient expression we find among the writings of the
prophets: "The fathers have eaten sour grapes, and the children's teeth
are set on edge."

Daniel Block, a biblical scholar and author of the multivolume set
on the book of Ezekiel for *The New International Commentary of the
Old Testament,* provides the following observation regarding this ancient
proverb:

> Scholars have generally understood the proverb as a sarcastic
> and cynical mockery of the system of divine "righteousness" that
> would punish children for the guilt of their parents. This doc-
> trine of transgenerational accountability was widespread in the
> ancient Near East.[51]

Transgenerational accountability is a scholarly expression of what
we would refer to as a generational curse from Almighty God. Block
also stresses that this proverb was sarcastic and mocked what God had
warned them about in the Decalogue. In one sense, his comments bring
to light the reality of a generational downward spiral that accompanies
the integration of pagan precepts. There are spirits behind all occult/
pagan practices. Once these spirits are given a foothold into a family
line, they begin their evil work. For now, let's return to Heaven's response
before dealing with Hell's denizens.

Ezekiel prophetically saw a day when Heaven would no longer move
in such a way against the unfaithful's future generations.

> The word of the LORD came to me again, saying, "What do you
> mean when you use this proverb concerning the land of Israel,
> saying: 'The fathers have eaten sour grapes, and the children's
> teeth are set on edge'? As I live," says the Lord GOD, "you shall
> no longer use this proverb in Israel. (Ezekiel 18:1–3)

Rather than reading through the entire chapter of Ezekiel 18 in this book, I want to jump to the prophetic punchline. (I do encourage you to read it in its entirety on your own.)

"Yet you say, 'The way of the Lord is not fair.' Hear now, O house of Israel, is it not My way which is fair, and your ways which are not fair? When a righteous man turns away from his righteousness, commits iniquity, and dies in it, it is because of the iniquity which he has done that he dies. Again, when a wicked man turns away from the wickedness which he committed, and does what is lawful and right, he preserves himself alive. Because he considers and turns away from all the transgressions which he committed, he shall surely live; he shall not die. Yet the house of Israel says, 'The way of the Lord is not fair.' O house of Israel, is it not My ways which are fair, and your ways which are not fair? Therefore I will judge you, O house of Israel, every one according to his ways," says the Lord GOD. "Repent, and turn from all your transgressions, so that iniquity will not be your ruin. Cast away from you all the transgressions which you have committed, and get yourselves a new heart and a new spirit. For why should you die, O house of Israel? For I have no pleasure in the death of one who dies," says the Lord GOD. "Therefore turn and live!" (Ezekiel 18:25–32)

What would bring this turnaround in the attitude of God? It was Jeremiah who saw the reason: a New Covenant!

In those days they shall say no more: "The fathers have eaten sour grapes, and the children's teeth are set on edge. "But every one shall die for his own iniquity; every man who eats the sour grapes, his teeth shall be set on edge. "Behold, the days are coming, says the LORD, when I will make a new covenant with the house of Israel and with the house of Judah—not according to the covenant that I made with their fathers in the day that I took them by the hand to lead them out of the land of Egypt, My covenant which they broke, though I was a husband to them," says the LORD. "But this is the covenant that I will make with the house of Israel after those days," says the LORD: "I will put My law in their minds, and write it on their hearts; and I will be their God, and they shall be My people." (Jeremiah 31:29–33)

The establishment of the New Covenant, through the completed work of Jesus on the cross, changed the dynamic of judging future generations. When people accept the vicarious sacrifice of Jesus on their behalf, the slate is washed clean as far as Heaven is concerned. The cross became a divine barrier that would serve as a bulwark against transgenerational accountability. Paul went as far as to say that we have become new creatures through Christ:

Therefore, if anyone is in Christ, he is a new creation; old things have passed away; behold, all things have become new. (2 Corinthians 5:17)

Jeremiah and Ezekiel foresaw this powerful transition and so did Isaiah, but in a different way:

Who has believed our report? And to whom has the arm of the LORD been revealed? For He shall grow up before Him as a tender plant, and as a root out of dry ground. He has no form or comeliness; and when we see Him, there is no beauty that we should desire Him. He is despised and rejected by men, a Man of sorrows and acquainted with grief. And we hid, as it were, our faces from Him; He was despised, and we did not esteem Him. Surely He has borne our griefs and carried our sorrows; yet we esteemed Him stricken, smitten by God, and afflicted. But

He was wounded for our transgressions, He was bruised for our iniquities; the chastisement for our peace was upon Him, and by His stripes we are healed. (Isaiah 53:1–5)

Isaiah prophetically saw what would be accomplished through the sacrifice of the Lamb of God. The completed work of Christ dealt with both transgressions (sin) and iniquity. We will deal with the differences between these two concepts in just a little bit.

The Good News of the Gospel is that, with Heaven, our sins are forgiven; we've been adopted into the family of God; and we've been given authority to bring the Kingdom into manifestation in the First Heaven.

While Heaven forgives, Hell never forgets! Remember, there are two kingdoms and two laws that are exact opposites of each other. Satan has no mercy, and he is a legalist!

Then I heard a loud voice saying in heaven, "Now salvation, and strength, and the kingdom of our God, and the power of His Christ have come, for the accuser of our brethren, who accused them before our God day and night, has been cast down. (Revelation 12:10)

Many Christians are surprised to learn that Lucifer's name was not changed to "Satan" after his fall from God's grace. "Satan" is a title, not a name. In broad terms, any fallen spirit that has aligned itself with Lucifer can be a "Satan," or "Adversary." Lucifer's entire kingdom shares that designation; they all have taken an adversarial role against God, His Kingdom, and humanity. In a narrower definition, *haSatan* (in Hebrew) means "prosecuting attorney." If you went to Israel today, you would find the title *haSatan* on the door of any prosecuting attorney in that country. Satan is a legalist. If he can find a legal right to access your life and create chaos, he will do it. He will not leave on his own, nor will he show any mercy. Not only is he a prosecuting attorney, but he is also an expert strategist. There are times when he will lie in wait with his legal right to move against you, until a strategic point is reached that will create the most damage.

In *The Shinar Directive*, I examined Ezekiel's prophetic expose of Lucifer:

> The first thing God said about Lucifer was, "Thou sealest up the sum." To understand exactly what God was saying here, we need to look at the Hebrew word used for "sum." *Tokniyth* (tokneeth') means "measurement, pattern, proportion." Lucifer was the seal; the pattern of perfect measurement. Then God used the word "wisdom." In Hebrew, the word is *chokmah* (khok-maw'), which means "wisdom, skill in war, wisdom in administration, shrewdness, prudence in religious affairs, and wisdom in ethical and religious matters."[52]

Lucifer possesses the seal of perfection as a warrior and a strategist. Remember, he was so cunning and powerful that one-third of the angels (who have seen the face of Almighty God and were present when He created the universe) believed Lucifer could win and followed him. Yet, despite all that the Word of God has revealed regarding the scope of his abilities, modern Christians have either been taught that he does not exist or that he is now powerless and has become a buffoon. In our warfare against the kingdom of darkness, these lies have us playing "Charismatic Candy Land" in Lucifer's minefields. Our paradigm must change. We must develop a Kingdom warrior's mindset.

In many ways, we find similarities between ourselves and the ancient Israelites a redeemer freed from slavery in Egypt. While we were in bondage, the squatters moved into our Promised Land and took over. Just because the Israelites were freed for Egypt does not mean that the giants and all the pagans who filled the Promised Land packed up their bags and left the land. *These agents of the mystery religions had to be driven out!*

Before we proceed, I want to spend some time defining the concepts of "sin" and "iniquity," then link them back to the Decalogue. God did not call the worship of other gods a sin (including the incorporation of pagan practices); He called it iniquity!

Understanding the Nature of Iniquity

A "sin" (or a "transgression") is a single act of sin. Sin can become "iniquity" if we're involved in sin long enough. "Iniquity" is the bending of a personality toward a particular sin or group of sins. In Isaiah's vision of the work of Messiah in Isaiah 53, have you ever wondered why Jesus was "wounded for transgressions" but "bruised for iniquity"? Sins are forgiven by the shedding of His divine blood. However, since iniquity is a twisting of the nature of an individual, if it was straightened, bruising would occur. We can see the same concept regarding the anointing of the Holy Spirit.

> It shall come to pass in that day that his burden will be taken away from your shoulder, and his yoke from your neck, and the yoke will be destroyed because of the anointing oil. (Isaiah 10:27)

Years ago, I heard a charismatic minister who was teaching on Isaiah 10:27 proclaim that the Hebrew word for "destroy" meant the yoke would disintegrate. However, that isn't really what the Hebrew word means. The Hebrew for "destroy" is *chabal* (*khaw-bal'*). While that term can mean "to destroy, corrupt, and ruin," it also means "to writhe, twist, and travail."[53] Imagine for a moment that an individual has been twisted up spiritually in some type of iniquity. He has been in this yoke for so long that it has distorted the very shape of his nature to come in line with the contours of his entrapment. Then, the anointing of God begins to work on his behalf. The anointing causes the yoke to twist (or untwist, if you will) and begins to affect the individual as well. His nature begins to return to its original shape. The yoke loses its grip on him, and he pulls free. Now, being free of Hell's yoke, the anointing continues its work in restoring him to his state before the bondage had been introduced. This untwisting of iniquity in his nature is the work of the Holy Spirit to restore the image of God within his soul. The original image had been marred by the talons of the enemy's grip. Paul reminds us that we all have our appointment with the anointing and the restoration of God's image upon our souls.

> For whom He foreknew, He also predestined to be conformed
> to the image of His Son, that He might be the firstborn among
> many brethren." (Romans 8:29)

Because we haven't been taught our responsibility to work with God and to yield to His mighty hand, we end up like Jacob of old. Our old nature formed in the image of the yoke that once imprisoned us begins to fight against the hand of God. We end up in a wrestling match with the Most High. But, like He did in the story of Jacob, rest assured that God will prevail. The twist to this story, if you will, is how long you will allow the marring in you to resist God instead of teaming up with the Almighty in the work of your transformation.

The Intoxicating Nature of the Nectar of Babylon

The mystery religions, paganism, and the occult have a spiritual dynamic that sin by itself does not possess. Involvement in the worship of other gods invokes their involvement and participation. Sometimes this worship isn't what we would normally consider as worship. It could involve oaths at one of their altars (such as in Freemasonry), using magic or sorcery for financial gain, or turning circumstances around in our favor. Sometimes, it can involve a secularized holiday that has its origins in the occult, such as Halloween. A spiritual infection occurs from the very first action taken. Throughout the First Covenant (Old Testament), "leaven" always referred to involvement in paganism and the occult. A little involvement would eventually take over everything. It wasn't until Jesus and the Gospel that Heaven was ever referred to as "leaven." I am sure the Lord's reference to Heaven as "leaven" (Matthew 13:33) was shocking to those who originally heard His preaching. It was a real game-changer. If you let Jesus in, He will never be satisfied until He is Lord of your entire life!

Whenever we are involved with any occult, pagan, or mystery religion practice, it opens the door to the ancient gods that established that practice. Magic or sorcery can go all the way back to the Watchers and Nephilim. Once a door is open, these fallen spirits will claim the individual and their bloodline. Because of the terminology used in the Decalogue, establishing a claim on a family line can expand to three or four generations. This concept can be seen in the masonic apron worn by Freemasons. It places the symbols for the god of the lodge right over the male's reproductive organ, thus claiming his offspring.

Masonic apron

Once given entrance, whether knowingly or unknowingly, these familiar spirits will place a spiritual claim on a family line. Their hold cannot be easily or flippantly broken; they must be driven out. Make no mistake here. Their altars (habits, beliefs, and attitudes they established in the family—i.e., strongholds) must be overturned, any objects involved in their invoking must be destroyed, and reliance upon them must be renounced. This will be warfare, because they will not give up easily. They will even attempt retaliation to bring the individual or family back to the place of reliance upon them.

Over the years, I have seen this same pattern. When people are saved, they are spiritual "babies." Heaven usually extends two to three years of grace, allowing them time to grow, become disciplined in the Word of God, and gain spiritual strength for the fight. Like the Israelites of old, they will eventually have to cross over the Jordan and face their giants. In generations past, the conversion process at salvation was longer than a thirty-second prayer. Ministries allowed the time necessary for the Holy Spirit to do His work. Sometimes, people spent hours at the altar getting right with God. I remember the stories in my family regarding my Grandfather Savage. Although he passed away before I was born, I've been told of how he came to faith in Christ. After a long struggle at the altar, he stood up as a completely different man. Even his countenance was changed that day. In our microwave-speed conversions today, many folks have half-cooked sessions of repentance, wherein they don't pray through to victory. It's sad to say, because of an assembly-line mentality, this culture has produced many unsaved "believers." Entering salvation is not a quick decision; it comes after a time of wrestling with God. Only after wrestling with God all night did Jacob rise as a different man and receive a new name! While I've already shared that "Israel" means "God prevails," it also has another meaning. It is a composite of two Hebrew words for "wrestle" and "God." Because Jacob had wrestled with God and God prevailed, Jacob's name was changed. Do we really think we can be grafted into Israel (Romans 11:11–36) without wrestling with God? It's time that we return to a biblical model and allow the Almighty time to transform hearts, minds, and lives!

Discipleship is a continuation of this wrestling. Once we're saved, how we think and view the world around us—and even our interpersonal relationships—aren't yet renewed to Kingdom standards. We still think like slaves to the kingdom of darkness. The Church is not a center for entertainment; it's a gym that trains believers to wrestle with their old ways, belief systems, and habits—and prevail! This is where generational tendencies are brought to bear and overcome.

> Now the Spirit expressly says that in latter times some will depart from the faith, giving heed to deceiving spirits and doctrines of demons, (1 Timothy 4:1)

I've spent over forty years training students for Gospel ministry. At many seminars, I have asked young aspirants and bishops alike what the "doctrines of demons" are in 1 Timothy 4:1. In all of those years, only one man answered correctly. The Apostle Paul uses the Greek word for "doctrines," *didaskalia* (did-as-kal-ee'-ah), which means "teaching, instruction; teaching; that which is taught, doctrine; teachings, precepts."[54] When we think of doctrine, we tend to gravitate to the modern concept of doctrinal statements or creeds. However, in the Hebraic setting in which the New Testament was written, it means something completely different. We've already dealt with the Torah's true meaning: instruction on how to walk with God. We've discovered that Hell has its own Torah. Doctrine is instruction on how to live, not just on how to believe. Before we come to Christ, the demonic taskmasters of Hell teach us their lies: how to live under their control, view the world, and interact with those around us. Their half-truths and outright lies are designed to keep us in bondage and under their control.

A vital aspect of engaging in spiritual warfare is confronting those lies within our souls, overcoming them with truth, and establishing new mindsets.

For though we walk in the flesh, we do not war according to the flesh. For the weapons of our warfare are not carnal but mighty in God for pulling down strongholds, casting down arguments and every high thing that exalts itself against the knowledge of God, bringing every thought into captivity to the obedience of Christ, and being ready to punish all disobedience when your obedience is fulfilled. (2 Corinthians 10:3–6)

We've already covered that the main definition of authority (*exousia*) is "the power of choice."[55] Only through the complete work of Christ are we placed in a position of power to examine our belief systems, under the direction of the Holy Spirit, to call out the lies we've been led to believe and reject them.

Throughout our lives, especially in the formative years of our childhood, the enemy has used individuals in bondage to plant his lies into the basic operating system of our souls. Whether it was physical or emotional abuse by others, the lies these events teach us were written into our unconscious minds and slowly became the lens through which we viewed ourselves and the world.

Anatomy of Footholds and Strongholds
In an article on defeating footholds and strongholds, Dr. Neil Anderson provides a solid working definition of a "spiritual foothold."

We overcome Satan's schemes when we understand how he oppresses us and how we must defeat him. Here are some clear ways to recognize demonic oppression in your life and find victory!
The evil one and his demons seize opportunities to cunningly influence our thinking in many different ways and to

varying degrees. If his schemes remain hidden from our conscience thought, they can form a foothold or establish a stronghold in our souls from which evil spirits can operate unimpeded.

Footholds

The most common use of the word "foothold" today is to describe a place or thing that will support a climber's foot or to denote a secure starting position from which further advancement can be made. In biblical Greek, it can refer to a spot, place, location, room, home, position, tract, occasion, opportunity, locality, region, or condition.

Paul gives us insight on how Satan might establish a foothold in our thinking from which further advancement can be made:

"In your anger do not sin": Do not let the sun go down while you are still angry, and do not give the devil a foothold. (Ephesians 4:26–27)

With these words, Paul warns us to quickly forgive an offense so that retained anger does not turn into bitterness, because bitterness (longheld unforgiveness) gives Satan a "foot up" in our thought life. It can give him a platform that will support further incursions into our thought life. [56]

Every event in which the enemy uses someone to affect us in a negative manner can give him a foothold in our lives if we don't respond properly. The disciples of Jesus saw that He approached life differently. He could always give comfort when needed, but He also rebuked others in love. They noted as well that when He prayed, Heaven always responded (and so did Hell)! They also saw the (unsuccessful) track record of the prayer life of the religious leaders in their day. So, they asked Jesus to teach them how to pray. In the words that came to be called the Lord's Prayer, Jesus' instruction featured an unusual sequence about forgiveness. Let's spend a few moments examining His words.

And forgive us our debts, as we forgive our debtors. (Matthew 6:12)

The Greek word used for "as" is an interesting one. *Kai* (*kahee*) cannot only be translated "as," but also as "when." In fact, *kai* is translated as "when" forty-two times in the KJV New Testament.[57] Whether it is translated as "as" or "when," the effects of following Jesus' teachings in the matter on the believer's prayer life are mind-boggling! Daily, it seems from the Gospels, Jesus was embroiled in ongoing debate with various factions of religious leaders in Judea. Most leaders saw Jesus as a threat to their position or influence in the Jewish community. It would be easy for hurt feelings to form. Imagine for a moment engaging in a debate with the One who had spoken the Torah to Moses about what the Torah taught. It would be easy to see how frustration and hurt feelings would have been a daily struggle for anyone. Jesus incorporated the concept of daily forgiving anyone who has wronged us as a "must do" in our prayer life—so much so that He connected it with our forgiveness from God. This wasn't the only occasion Messiah taught this truth. One day, Jesus answered a question by Peter with a parable on the Kingdom of God:

Then Peter came to Him and said, "Lord, how often shall my brother sin against me, and I forgive him? Up to seven times?" Jesus said to him, "I do not say to you, up to seven times, but up to seventy times seven. Therefore the kingdom of heaven is like a certain king who wanted to settle accounts with his servants. And when he had begun to settle accounts, one was brought to him who owed him ten thousand talents. But as he was not able to pay, his master commanded that he be sold, with his wife and children and all that he had, and that payment be made. The servant therefore fell down before him, saying, 'Master, have patience with me, and I will pay you all.' Then the master of that servant was moved with compassion, released him, and forgave him the debt. But that servant went out and found one of his fellow servants who owed him a hundred denarii; and he laid hands on him and took him by the throat, saying, 'Pay me what you owe!' So his fellow servant fell down at his feet and begged him, saying, 'Have patience with me, and I will pay you all.' And he would not, but went and threw him into prison till he should pay the debt. So when his fellow servants saw what had been done, they were very grieved, and came and told their master all that had been done. Then his master, after he had called him, said to him, 'You wicked servant! I forgave you all that debt because you begged me. Should you not also have had compassion on your fellow servant, just as I had pity on you?" And his master was angry, and delivered him to the torturers until he should pay all that was due to him. So My heavenly Father also will do to you if each of you, from his heart, does not forgive his brother his trespasses." (Matthew 18:21–35)

Unforgiveness, among many other things, can give the enemy a foothold. (Remember my story of having to deal with infiltrators while in the military in Europe. Infiltration can be accomplished through seduction, coercion, or blackmail. Each one of these manipulations can give the operator a foothold in the target's life.) Any foothold is the beginning of a stronghold. Jesus knew what His disciples would face in the years ahead. His teachings on the model prayer are essential for all believers to understand. Remember, while we are on the field of battle (i.e., planet earth), everything that goes on is spiritual warfare. When everything inside of us is screaming for revenge or even justice, choosing to forgive is an act of spiritual warfare. When we strategically forgive (usually the most painful events), we pull the rug out from under the enemy's schemes for our lives.

A foothold serves as an entry point or a base camp to set up operations for an invasion. A stronghold is an entirely different situation. A stronghold is a fort or fortress. There are residents who dwell in the fortified area the enemy has constructed within our souls. I've read many books on spiritual warfare and each one speaks of strongholds, but none deal with the reality that a stronghold is a place where something/someone lives. Jesus called them "tormenters." These tormenters feed off both the torment they bring to our lives and the torment we become in the lives of those around us. These unwelcome squatters not only bring pain and hardship (until we see the truth), but convince us to stand guard over and come to depend on the fortified stronghold to cope with the world. Another tactic these tormenters use is to convince us that their feelings (or perversions) are ours instead of their tacit influence. This causes us not only to accept their influence, but to fight to keep—and justify—whatever sin they manifest through us.

An Example from My Own Life

I've shared on occasions that my childhood wasn't a pleasant one. My stepfather, who later adopted me (I took his last name), had a low IQ—probably somewhere between 85 and 95. Every day, he would faithfully purchase our local newspaper in St. Louis and spend hours poring over it. I didn't discover until I was an adult that he only had an elementary reading level and barely understood what he was attempting to read. He was easily frustrated by situations and circumstances, and his frustration always turned into anger. Like in most domestic violence cases, he was jovial in public. However, in private, he was a different person. As an only child (his children resided with his ex-wife, and his four sons would have little to do with him), I found myself in the crosshairs of his anger any time we were alone. Any little thing would set him off. Sometimes, he would make up something as an excuse to enter his hate-filled tirades. Sometimes these tongue lashings would last for an hour or more. But, like clockwork, these verbal bouts would end about ten minutes before my mother returned home from work. It gave me time to settle back down, allowing him to pretend nothing had happened. I was even threatened on the night I was saved. I had attended church with my best friend (Leroy), and it was after the service that I accepted Christ's sacrifice and made Jesus my Lord and Savior. When I returned home and shared the news, I was threatened with the strap for having the audacity to get saved when my parents weren't present.

Day after day, his own woundedness and the demonic forces that fed his anger began creating a narrative of self-hatred, self-sabotage, feelings of worthlessness, and defeat in my unconscious mind. His words of "you will never amount to anything" and "you are stupid and worthless" became the unconscious script of my life—even after I accepted the call to ministry on my thirteenth birthday. Shortly after my wife, Mary, and I were married, we attended a meeting in which the pastor had invited an extraordinarily clear and accurate prophetic minister—unlike those who pass today as being prophetic. The speaker's words were a gentle blending of prophetic insight, divine correction, and hope. I remember sitting there in amazement as we listened. At that time, the prophet called Mary and me out with a prophetic word for each of us. Here is a summation of the words we received that day.

To me: "Young man, do you know you are called to ministry? Your calling is unusually strong and something I have rarely seen. Your ministry is going to affect the world."

To Mary: "Your part in this ministry is to pray it into existence."

Mary and I sat there shocked. We smiled and may have even nodded our heads in agreement. Yet, if we were truthful, on the inside we were saying "Yeah, right!" Mary and I were the farthest thing from what the prophet described that day. Our inner dialogue was taking us in the opposite direction, which is what Hell wanted all along. Even more than that, it caused us to question, and for me, to even reject, at times, what was spoken.

Over a decade later, I was frustrated with the ministry (and life in general). Complaining to God about the situation, I even brought up the prophetic words Mary and I had received. At that moment, the Holy Spirit interrupted my fleshly gripe-fest. That day, I clearly heard from God. Here is what He said: "The prophetic word was true. But you are so strong-headed that it may take me another twenty years to make you into the man who can walk in that prophetic word."

That day, I realized the enemy had programmed me to fight against the very calling I had surrendered to when I was thirteen.

About six months later, I had a visitation from the Lord. I need to paint a picture for you to properly understand what happened that day. I was operating a seminary from a small house I rented in our neighborhood. It was right across the street from our home. In my office, any space that wasn't taken up by overstuffed bookshelves was covered in degrees I had earned, academic awards I had received, recognitions I had been given, and so forth. In retrospect, the setting in my office was more about convincing me of who I was supposed to be and not about validating myself to visitors. Sitting there, the words of my stepfather filled my mind and directed my feelings: I felt stupid and useless, and believed I would never achieve anything worthwhile for God. In those moments of despair, Jesus walked into the room. I could not see Him, but His presence was tangible. I remember sitting there typing away at my keyboard with tears running down my face. I felt the Lord walk up behind me and place His hands on my shoulders. There was such peace and a sense of holiness. I did not dare turn around. This is what the Lord said that day: "Your stepfather has spoken Hell's lies over your entire life. I am here to speak my truth into your life."

The Lord continued with both loving correction and affirmation. He spoke the absolute opposite of what had been spoken to me thousands of times. Those words were so personal, so precious, that I have not shared them with a living soul. They are too holy. I have only shared a small portion with Mary. In fact, tears are running down my face at this moment. Just thinking of this event is still so emotional for me. It is so holy.

Jesus' words washed over my mind and gave me strength. It also started me on a rocky road that has led me to where I am now. Many times I've had to take the words the Lord spoke over me to war against the hellish narrative that would occasionally rear its ugly head from my old way of thinking. This is one of the reasons that 2 Corinthians 10 is so real for me. The greatest battlefield that we will ever face is the one within. Sometimes, it will feel like a million wars have been waged on that battlefield. In the past, every battle may have been lost. Yet, when we bring God into the equation, the tide slowly turns. We gain the courage to call out the enemy's lies, bind them up, and reject them. We mustn't stop there! We must replace the enemy's lies with God's truth until the battlefield is transformed from a stronghold to a fortress of truth. I have found that it is essential to speak God's truth out loud in those struggles. Spoken words have power. Psychologically, the unconscious mind constantly seeks updated information. What we say aloud with conviction holds a higher priority for our unconscious mind than the lies spoken by others. We must combat the lies of the past by speaking God's truth until it has overwritten them. Here is an example:

I've been told that I will never amount to anything in this life. First, I declare those words as a lie of the enemy. The truth is in the Word, which says:

> For we are God's [own] handiwork (His workmanship), recreated in Christ Jesus, [born anew] that we may do those good works which God predestined [planned beforehand] for us [taking paths He prepared ahead of time], that we should walk in them [living the good life He prearranged and made ready for us to live]. (Ephesians 2:10, AMP)

Then, I command any spirits that have accompanied and empowered this lie to leave me now, in Jesus' name.

Next, I pray: Father, I have declared your truth over me. Empower my words by your Spirit. I plead with you for Jesus' protection over the areas of my mind that held those lies, and I ask that the blood He shed in His sacrifice on the cross would cleanse me. Give me your grace to walk in your truth, in Jesus' name.

Now the question is: How many times do we need to do this? How many times has a lie been spoken to us, and how many times did the enemy reinforce it? We declare it until it becomes a part of us. In this aspect of spiritual warfare, with each declaration of truth, we are battering the entrenched areas (strongholds, or fortresses) the enemy has skillfully built within our souls. We hit the stronghold until the walls are destroyed and the demonic spirits embedded in them are completely driven out of our lives. These strongholds were not built overnight, nor will they be completely demolished overnight. Remember, this is a fight, but the Lord has given us the victory!

We live in a continual battle while on earth. We must fight the temptation to practice unforgiveness. We must also always be on guard for the enemy's lies that seek to establish footholds within our souls. The enemy never plays fair. But we have an advantage that is revealed by the Apostle John.

> My little children, these things I write to you, so that you may not sin. And if anyone sins, we have an Advocate with the Father, Jesus Christ the righteous. And He Himself is the propitiation for our sins, and not for ours only but also for the whole world. (1 John 2:1–2)

I have already established that Satan operates as a prosecuting attorney in the court of the LORD. However, he isn't the only one who is there. In 1 John 2:1, John reveals that Jesus is our advocate. The Greek word John uses is another legal term. The Greek word for advocate is *parakletos* (*par-ak'-lay-tos*), which means:

> …summoned, called to one's side, esp. called to one's aid; one who pleads another's cause before a judge, a pleader, **counsel for defense**, legal assistant, an advocate; one who pleads another's cause with one, an intercessor; of Christ in his exaltation at God's right hand, pleading with God the Father for the pardon of our sins.[58] (Emphasis added)

Jesus is our Defense Attorney. Our Savior stands before the judgment seat of Almighty God, ready to plead our case based upon His completed work on our behalf. Not only is He our Defense Attorney, but He is also our Great Shepherd who is watching over us and who has filled us with His Spirit. He fills us on the inside, He stands to watch over us on the outside, and He stands for us before the heavenly court. We need to transition from Jacob (one who wrestled with God) to Israel (one who learned to lean on God). We will discover at that moment of transition that God has our best interest at heart, and He desires to work with us to assist us in overcoming the enemy.

Prayer

Father, I come to you in the powerful name of Jesus. I realize that, while I was lost, the enemy has made many strongholds in my life and has taught me many lies. I ask that you give me grace and allow me to move in authority to raze what the enemy has built within my soul.

As an act of my will, I choose to forgive anyone who has hurt me, whether physically or emotionally. I submit those areas to you for healing and restoration. I ask that your Spirit reveal anything hidden that needs to be resolved in my soul. I will choose to forgive and allow the blood of Jesus to cleanse and restore those areas. I also ask that you forgive me of my sins and the sins of my fathers (Nehemiah 1:6). I stand in the authority that has been given to me by Jesus, and I command any spirits that have gained access to my life through my sins or through the sins of my ancestors to leave me now. Your legal right has been removed by the blood of Jesus. I now stand before my Heavenly Father's court and ask for divine assistance in driving the kingdom of darkness from my life. Since I have asked forgiveness for the sins of myself and my ancestors, I declare that any spirits cannot transfer to any of my descendants. My bloodline now belongs to Almighty God. I also bind up any retaliatory efforts of the enemy because of the declarations I have made today, and I release the power of the Kingdom of God to enforce the binding.

Father, I invite your Spirit to assist me in renewing my mind. Reveal any strongholds that need to be pulled down. Reveal the lies of the enemy that I accepted long ago (even as a small child) and help me replace those lies with your truth. I will not rest until every stronghold has been pulled down and every thought has been made subject to the Lordship of Jesus.

Father, please work with me to overcome all of the machinations of the enemy so I can live a life that proclaims your glory, power, and truth of the Gospel to the world around me. Help me to carry the name of Jesus with integrity and honor on earth. In Jesus' name.

Review Questions

1. In Numbers 14, we find that Israel did something unthinkable toward God. What was it, and what was the penalty for their actions?
2. In the Decalogue, God warned Israel that there would be transgenerational consequences for involvement in pagan and occult practices. According to the prophets, what spiritual dynamic changed Heaven's response?
3. What is spiritual adultery?
4. While Heaven forgives, Hell never _____.
5. In Revelation 12:10, what is Satan revealed as?

6. In referring to Lucifer in Ezekiel, what do the Hebrew words *tokniyth* and *chokmah* reveal?

7. How is iniquity different from sin?

8. How does the anointing affect the yoke of iniquity?

9. Mystery religions, paganism, and the occult have a spiritual dynamic that sin, by itself, does not possess. What is it?

10. What are the doctrines of demons?

11. What is the difference between footholds and strongholds?

12. Who are the tormenters?

13. How do we pull down the strongholds of the enemy?

14. What is the unconscious mind always looking for?

15. In 1 John 2:1–2, the Apostle John reveals an important aspect of Jesus' current ministry in our lives. What is He revealed as?

GOING DEEPER

Generational Tendencies and How to Overcome Them

> Do not be conformed to this world (this age), [fashioned after and adapted to its external, superficial customs], but be transformed (changed) by the [entire] renewal of your mind [by its new ideals and its new attitude], so that you may prove [for yourselves] what is the good and acceptable and perfect will of God, even the thing which is good and acceptable and perfect [in His sight for you].
>
> ROMANS 12:2 (AMP)

There is great debate within the psychological community regarding behavior: Are behavioral tendencies genetic or environmental? Our Greco-Roman mindset forces us into a linear logic that requires us to settle on one answer. The Hebraic mindset, which forms the entire backdrop for the Word of God, is not linear; it is "block logic." In other words, two diametrically opposing truths can sit side by side in dynamic tension. (An example would be the free will of humanity and the sovereignty of God. As far as I can tell, neither Calvin nor Arminius was trained in Semitic thought.) So, generational tendencies can be both environmental and genetic. The environment can reinforce the genetic tendencies that are empowered by spiritual forces (good or bad).

There is evidence that behavior can be encoded in our genetics. While scientists tell us they have completely decoded the human genome, there are large sections of our DNA considered "junk" DNA. They claim these sections of ancient genetic code are leftovers of the evolutionary process. I believe their postulation is science-speak for "I don't have a clue as to why it's there." Other researchers will look at some aspects of this so-called junk code and see remnants of our souls. There is growing evidence in some quarters that the behavioral traits within families can be found in their DNA. If this is true, it could explain how iniquity is passed from generation to generation. The spiritual twisting toward certain sins may be genetic and environmental. Not only is that leaning toward certain sins there, but they are learned through the dysfunctional behavior of the family unit.

At this point, it would be easy to give up. If it is in my genetic code, there is no way of correcting it. However, behavioral and physical aspects can be altered when speaking of DNA. We are discovering that constantly reinforced behavior can turn genes in our DNA on or off. Those in the occult have known about the ability to turn genes on and off for centuries (well before humanity even knew DNA existed). This is why adepts in the occult are so disciplined. They attempt to activate or deactivate some aspects of their genetics. Some researchers speculate that their discipline is designed to reactive some dormant Nephilim aspect of their DNA or even what has been dubbed "the Lucifer gene."[59] Looking at the information I provided, your first response may be thinking I have gone off the deep end. However, a whole new branch of science is developing around this very concept. This science is known as epigenetics. (Caspar McCloud is a good friend, colleague, and pastor who has written an excellent book on epigenetics from a Christian perspective. His book is entitled, *What Was I Thinking? Getting Your Thoughts to Work for You Instead of against You.* This outstanding book should be in every believer's library.)

An example would be someone with a healthy bloodline who develops a sedentary lifestyle. Over time, this new behavior that has been introduced (the low level of activity) can turn off specific genes that will cause the individual (and their descendants) to become more susceptible to diseases like diabetes or heart disease. The good news is that developing an active lifestyle can turn those genes back on.

How we can "turn off" iniquity in a bloodline and "turn on" a bend toward God is the same process in which the iniquity was established in the first place. It usually follows this sequence:

1. A spiritual force introduces a new behavior into someone's life.
2. The new behavior is reinforced through the empowerment of the spiritual force and the individual's constant participation in that behavior.
3. Eventually, this new behavior becomes instinctual in the individual.

The enemy has been using epigenetics against humanity since the days of the Garden of Eden. It's time we begin using this process to replace the enemy's influence on our lives with the impact of the Kingdom of God.

Before we look at how this process can be reversed, we need to examine how environmental elements can affect our behavior and even our perceived identity.

Environmental Factors in Development

The family environment is a key area in which the enemy's lies can infect the next generation. We come into this world with the basic software of life installed. For the most part, this essential software works in the background and handles the body's unconscious functions. Everything else must be learned. Love must be learned. Joy and trust must be learned. Hatred, prejudice, and mistrust must be learned. The family unit is where we initially learn everything. Child development experts have stated that by the time children reach the age of five, they have learned 85– 90 percent of everything they will ever learn.[60] That's how much of a blank slate we are once we enter this world. Unfortunately, once we grow beyond five years of age, the neuroplasticity is significantly reduced, and much of what we've learned is moved to long-term storage in our unconscious mind. In other words, the lessons learned become part of how we see the world (and ourselves) and react to it on a subconscious level. Often, this will manifest as an emotion without a logical reason for why we feel that way.

So, the lessons previous generations learned from covert agents from the kingdom of darkness can be passed down through the family's worldview. It takes the completed work of Christ and the power of the Holy Spirit to overcome this generational programming.

Declaring War on the Enemy Within

For though we walk in the flesh, we do not war according to the flesh. For the weapons of our warfare *are* not carnal but mighty in God for pulling down strongholds, casting down arguments and every high thing that exalts itself against the knowledge of God, bringing every thought into captivity to the obedience of Christ, and being ready to punish all disobedience when your obedience is fulfilled. (2 Corinthians 10:3–6)

Worldly weapons will not work in a spiritual battle. We cannot use a firearm and arrest a vain imagination. No matter how well-trained we are in hand-to-hand combat, we cannot punch our way to victory. This warfare is entirely different: It is the war inside our minds.

Most individuals believe anything that pops into their heads. They've never been taught the truth about the battlefield of the soul. There are three sources of our thoughts, feelings, and actions:

1. The kingdom of darkness—including all of its agents of misery and chaos.
2. Ourselves—including both the old nature's carnal desires and the new nature's spiritual desires.
3. The Kingdom of God—including the Holy Spirit and all the divine agents of the King.

In my book, *The Sheeriyth Imperative*, I discuss the triune nature of the universe and humanity's design.

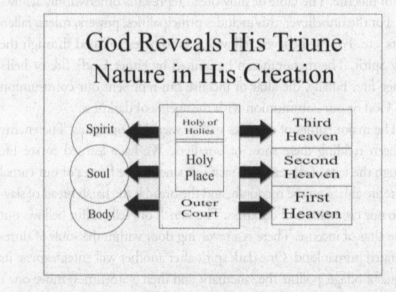

Let's examine the theological significance of the illustration I've provided. Our spirit person is the natural equivalent to the Holy of Holies in the Tabernacle.

Spirit: The throne of God dwells here, in our spirit. This truth is revealed in the example of the Tabernacle: the Ark of the Covenant represented the throne of God on earth. In the unsaved, their spirit is dead to God. Biblically, death is represented by separation. Our spirit and soul are separated from our physical bodies when we die physically. The unregenerated are dead, or separated from the Third Heaven. When we are born again, our spirit person is reborn, the throne of God is established there, and our spirit person directly connects to God's throne. The Holy Spirit then goes to work in our lives, and we gain the ability to walk in the Spirit instead of being led constantly by our souls. Although this ability is in the design of every believer, most of us aren't taught how to develop this walk from our spirit nature outward. However, this should be a part of discipleship in the Body of Christ.

Souls: Our souls are represented by the Holy Place. There are three items in the Holy Place: the table of showbread, the menorah, and the altar of incense. The table of showbread represents otherworldly fellowship. For the unbeliever, this includes principalities, powers, rulers, fallen spirits, etc. For the believer, fellowship is to be established through the Holy Spirit. The menorah can be ignited by either God's fire or hell's strange fire. Finally, the altar of incense can represent our communion with God or our communion with the agents of darkness.

The major battles of our lives will be waged in our souls. The enemy has been residing there most of our lives. We have learned to see life through the lens of the enemy's tacit influences. The flames of our carnal nature are ablaze on the menorah, and the bread is the harsh bread of slavery to our taskmasters of darkness. The stench of Hell's sulfur bellows out of the altar of incense. There is a revolving door within the souls of unregenerated humankind. One dark spirit after another will enter, express its unique bondage, pollute the sanctuary, and then (sometimes) move on.

Satan's Soul Market

There are several Greek words used in the New Testament that are translated as "redemption." In his book, *Dressed to Kill: A Biblical Approach to Spiritual Warfare and Armor*, Greek scholar and author Rick Renner provides great insight into two of these Greek words that are paramount to our current study.

> God sent His Son into the enemy's "slave market" with one purpose in mind: so Jesus could secure man's deliverance from Satan's bondage once and for all! It was into this stinking, deteriorating, sinking, death-permeated, demonically energized world, where all of humankind was being auctioned off by the devil into various kinds of slavery and bondage, that Jesus Christ came 2,000 years ago. And God sent His Son into the enemy's "slave market" with one purpose in mind: so Jesus could secure man's deliverance from Satan's bondage once and for all! *Agoridzo*, translated "redemption" in the New Testament, denotes this horrible, deplorable, abject slavery in Satan's slave market where we used to live. But, thank God, we don't live there anymore!
>
> The word *agoridzo*, fully understood in the context of "redemption," means that Jesus came to redeem us from this miserable state of bondage. As Paul told the Corinthians, "For ye are bought with a price..." (1 Corinthians 6:20). The word "bought" in this verse is the word *agoridzo*. Regarding this same redeeming work of Jesus, Paul said again later, "Ye are bought with a price; be not ye the servants of men" (1 Corinthians 7:23). The word "bought" is once again derived from the word *agoridzo*. Paul's admonition could be paraphrased: "Since Jesus paid the price to deliver you from bondage and slavery to Satan, do not now turn around and make yourselves slaves to people!" When the 24 elders fall before the throne of God and begin to worship, they sing a song about Jesus' work of redeeming us from Satan's slave market: "And they sung a new song, saying, Thou art worthy to take the book, and to open the seals thereof:

for thou wast slain, and hast redeemed [*agoridzo*] us to God by thy blood out of every kindred, and tongue, and people, and nation" (Revelation 5:9). It is imperative for us to understand the word *agoridzo*. This important word adequately portrays our spiritually bankrupt condition in the "slave market" of the world before Jesus Christ set us free, as well as Jesus' redemptive work to remove us from that terrible place. This leads us to the second word for "redemption" that is used in the New Testament. PUR-CHASED "OUT OF" SLAVERY. The second Greek word for "redemption" is derived from the word *exagoridzo*. The word *exagoridzo* is a compound of the words *ex* and *agoridzo*. The word *ex* is a preposition that means out and, as we have already discussed, the word *agoridzo* described a slave market. When *ex* and *agoridzo* are combined, they form the word *exagoridzo*, which pictures one who has come to purchase a slave OUT OF the slave market.

Exagoridzo conveys the idea of removal. Therefore, it signi-fies the purchase of a slave in order to permanently set that slave FREE from that heinous place, never to be put on the trading block of slavery again. The word *exagoridzo* pictures a slave who has been liberated out of that stinking, nauseating, disgusting, depraved, and cursed slave market forever![61]

While we were in slavery to the kingdom of darkness, the enemy converted the Holy Place into a slave market. The new believer's task is to cleanse the soul through the washing of the water of the Word and the power of the Holy Spirit to restore the holiness of this sanctuary within. This holy task is not always so easily accomplished. These unholy task-masters have trained us to see life through their eyes, think that their hellish desires are our own, and even depend on their instruction to navigate life's obstacles. It takes a warrior's heart to have the courage to reject everything we've been trained by Hell to think and feel, then replace it with God's loving instructions.

Our Weapons of Warfare

In 1 Corinthians 10 (NKJV), we read that our weapons are "mighty in God" to pull down the enemy's strongholds. When I examined the original Greek text through *Logos Bible Software*, in its word-by-word, original-language analysis, I found the phrase translated as "divinely powerful to the destruction of fortresses."

The Greek word used for "mighty" is *dunatos* (*doo-nat-os*). Liddell's *A Greek-English Lexicon* defines this word as "strong, mighty; the ablest-bodied men; sound in limb; fit for service; powerful." [62] By adding the Greek word *theo* to *dunatos*, Paul was describing God's might that is released on the inside of the believer. Like Israel, we must depend on God's strength, not on our ability. To be honest, I think we've greatly underestimated the power of God to fight the battle within. The enemy has us focused on the battle in the physical world, which distracts us from the real battle. If believers ever win the battle within, they become weapons firmly in the hands of God to serve as an engine of change in the world. The enemy fears this transformation more than we can ever imagine. The kingdom of darkness is still reeling under the power of what 120 believers started on the day of Pentecost more than two thousand years ago. Imagine for a moment what would be possible if millions of believers won the war within and were free to wage the battle without. As we enter the final conflict, this dynamic will become a reality, resulting in the last harvest of souls for the Kingdom of God. But for now, let's return to our discussion of winning the battle within.

Neuroplasticity and the New Birth

There is something supernatural about the new birth. While that may be the understatement of the millennium, there is a truth here we have yet to grasp. Remember our discussion about the first five years of life for a newborn? The neuroplasticity in those years is nothing short of a miracle. Little brains are sponges that soak up everything around them. When we are born -again, the Holy Spirit restores our spiritual neuroplasticity. We're supercharged to learn the ways of the Kingdom. We are hungry for learning God's truth, discovering His ways, and finding out how to be led by His Spirit. Yet, instead of being biblically trained to walk with God, we're indoctrinated to interact with the religious cultures we've created within our denominations and movements. These cultures are a blending of small portions of the ways of God, the doctrines of men, and the spiritual drift that occurs over time. We've all seen the spiritual drift that happens in denominations and movements that were once on fire for God: Now that once-holy fire is nothing but tiny embers. What's worse, that in some movements, the fire of God has been replaced by the strange fire of Mystery Babylon. For those in ministry, we need to examine the protocols we have in place for new believers. Are we giving them the support system they need? Are there discipleship programs that take advantage of this spiritually supercharged learning curve to reeducate the mind to Kingdom principles? If we're going to meet the needs of the current generation, we need to rework every aspect of ministry to train and empower the Remnant.

With all this in mind, we may ask, "I was born again decades ago; where does this leave me?" Anytime we take our walk with God seriously and seek His fire in our lives, the Holy Spirit can open the door to a three-year window of neuroplasticity to rewire the brain for Kingdom living. Dr. Paul Hegstrom, a friend and graduate of the seminary where I was chancellor, specialized in ministering to those in situations of domestic violence. He discovered a power principle of the soul regarding the renewal of the mind. It takes three years of purposeful training to rewire the brain with new patterns of thought and behavior. He documented this discovery in his DVD, entitled *The Brain*. This concept is found in two places in Scripture:

1. When Daniel was trained to serve in the court of
    Nebuchadnezzar, the educational process took three years.

2. After Jesus confronted Paul on the road to Damascus, Paul spent three years in the desert in prayer and study. During this time, many believe Paul was taken up to the Third Heaven and trained by Jesus regarding the redemption of the Gentiles (2 Corinthians12:1–34). Theologically, this is called the Pauline Revelation.

We must move beyond the microwave/event mindset of the modern Church. There is not a prayer that I can come up with to instantaneously retrain our minds from worldly living (dominated by the kingdom of darkness) to Kingdom living. If someone is promising such a miracle, he or she is peddling snake oil. However, if we are willing to work with the Holy Spirit and invest the time necessary to renew our minds, there is a prayer that can *begin* the process. It requires patience. Our walk with the Lord is a life-long journey and not a sprint. Sometimes, the Holy Spirit needs to work with us and prepare us to see something before He can deal with it in our lives. There are no shortcuts.

Walking in Unreality or Reality?

The enemy always brings chaos. We find his first salvo in the second verse of Genesis 1:

The earth was without form, and void; and darkness was on the face of the deep. And the Spirit of God was hovering over the face of the waters. (Genesis 1:2)

The phrase "without form" in Genesis 1:2 is derived from the Hebrew word *tohuw* (to'-hoo). According to the *Enhanced Strong's Lexicon*, *tohuw* means "formlessness, confusion, unreality, emptiness."[63] Lucifer's fall brought unreality to our universe. In much the same way, when the taskmasters of Hell were dwelling in our souls, that's exactly

what they bring to our lives: unreality. We're not interacting with the
world around us based on reality (from God's point of view). Instead, we
are experiencing life through the lies, distortions, and unreality taught
in our families and by these demonic forces. The cure, of course, is the
completed work of Christ. One day, Jesus proclaimed:

> "If you abide in My word, you are My disciples indeed. And you
> shall know the truth, and the truth shall make you free." [The
> believing Jews] answered Him, "We are Abraham's descendants,
> and have never been in bondage to anyone. How can you say,
> 'You will be made free'?" Jesus answered them, "Most assuredly,
> I say to you, whoever commits sin is a slave of sin. And a slave
> does not abide in the house forever, but a son abides forever.
> Therefore if the Son makes you free, you shall be free indeed.
> (John 8:31b–36)

I want to point out several ideas about these verses. First, let's deal with
the word "truth." In the original Greek, the word for "truth" is *aletheia*
(*al-ay'-thi-a*), which means "objectively, what is true in any matter under
consideration; truly, in truth, according to truth, of a truth, in reality."[64]
Remember, Jesus is Almighty God who has come in the flesh. His Word
begins in Genesis 1:1 and ends in Revelation 27:20. God's Word is not
only truth, but reality. It is the only cure for the unreality of the enemy.
What did the Creator do that turned the tide in the chaos and unreality
that was released on planet earth? He spoke to it! His Word restored reality.

The Apostle Paul was sharing a divine mystery with the believers
in Ephesus. He used the analogy of marriage to reveal a greater truth:
the dynamic of Christ and the Church. Let's look at those verses in
Ephesians 5:

> Husbands, love your wives, just as Christ also loved the church
> and gave Himself for her, that He might sanctify and cleanse her

with the washing of water by the word, that He might present her to Himself a glorious church, not having spot or wrinkle or any such thing, but that she should be holy and without blemish. (Ephesians 5:25–27)

The washing of the Word extinguishes the carnal flame on the menorah of the soul and replaces it with the fire of God. The water of the Word drives out the enemy's filth in our souls and replaces it with God's reality—His truth. Have we learned how to use the sword of the Spirit (the Word of God) fight against the lies of the enemy that were established in our souls? Over the years, I have reminded believers that the sword of the Spirit is two-edged: one side is for the war within and the other side is for the war without.

When we are born again, the transformation of the soul from being in a hellish slave market to residing in the Holy Place doesn't happen automatically. Like the Israelites crossing over the Jordan and driving out the giants in the Promised Land, we must roll up our sleeves and labor with the Holy Spirit to cleanse our souls from the wretched effects of the enemy and claim our lives for the Kingdom of God alone! When the Apostle Paul said to "bring every thought into captivity to Christ" 2 Corinthians 10:5) he outlined the primary battlefield of our warfare. We ignore his instruction at our own peril.

Spiritual Genetics and Environmental Behaviors Combined

Almighty God knew all the dynamics we have covered before the foundation of the world. Wouldn't it seem logical for Him to bring both aspects—spiritual genetics and environmental behaviors—together in His people's redemptive and sanctification process? We've already covered how our genes can be altered by spiritual forces working in tandem with individuals:

- A spiritual force introduces a new behavior into someone's life.
- The new behavior is reinforced through the empowerment of the spiritual force and the individual's constant participation in that behavior.
- Eventually, this new behavior becomes instinctual in the individual.
- This dynamic works both ways.

Hear, O Israel: The LORD our God, the LORD is one! You shall love the LORD your God with all your heart, with all your soul, and with all your strength. And these words which I command you today shall be in your heart. You shall teach them diligently to your children, and shall talk of them when you sit in your house, when you walk by the way, when you lie down, and when you rise up. You shall bind them as a sign on your hand, and they shall be as frontlets between your eyes. You shall write them on the doorposts of your house and on your gates. (Deuteronomy 6:4–9)

How do we show God that we love Him? First, we follow His commandments. Then we create a family atmosphere of regularly hearing them and carrying them out. Purposefully following the Kingdom instructions takes us through the doorway to blessings from God. I call this intentional Kingdom living. We kick ourselves out of neutral (living instinctively according to what has already been written in our unconscious minds) and examine our every thought and internal response to the situations in life. We respond to life's problems by purposefully following the Word in every case, whether we feel like it or not. Eventually, our emotional reactions will align with the instructions of the Word of God, and it will begin to feel unnatural to respond by our carnal nature. The writer of the book of Hebrews admonishes us regarding this transformation:

For though by this time you ought to be teachers, you need someone to teach you again the first principles of the oracles of God; and you have come to need milk and not solid food. For everyone who partakes only of milk is unskilled in the word of righteousness, for he is a babe. But solid food belongs to those who are of full age, that is, those who by reason of use have their senses exercised to discern both good and evil. (Hebrews 5:12–14)

Did you catch what the writer of Hebrews said in verse 14? Our senses (i.e., our soul and flesh) can be trained to discern both good and evil. Adam Clarke, in his commentary on the Bible, provides significant insight into this thought:

Have their senses exercised—The word αισθητηρια signifies the different organs of sense, as the eyes, ears, tongue, and palate, nose, and finger ends, and the nervous surface in general, through which we gain the sensations called seeing, hearing, tasting, smelling, and feeling. These organs of sense, being frequently exercised or employed on a variety of subjects, acquire the power to discern the various objects of sense: viz. all objects of light; difference of sounds; of tastes or savours; of odours or smelling; and of hard, soft, wet, dry, cold, hot, rough, smooth, and all other tangible qualities.

There is something in the soul that answers to all these senses in the body. And as universal nature presents to the other senses their different and appropriate objects, so religion presents to these interior senses the objects which are suited to them. Hence in Scripture we are said, even in spiritual things, to see, hear, taste, smell, and touch or feel. These are the means by which the soul is rendered comfortable, and through which it derives its happiness and perfection.

In the adult Christian these senses are said to be γεγυμνασμενα, exercised, a metaphor taken from the athlete or contenders in the Grecian games, who were wont to employ all their powers, skill, and agility in mock fights, running, wrestling, etc., that they might be the better prepared for the actual contests when they took place. So these employ and improve all their powers, and in using grace get more grace; and thus, being able to discern good from evil, they are in little danger of being imposed on by false doctrine, or by the pretensions of hypocrites; or of being deceived by the subtleties of Satan. They feel that their security depends, under God, on this exercise—on the proper use which they make of the grace already given them by God. Can any reader be so dull as not to understand this?[65]

If we will work with the Holy Spirit to cleanse the soul (the Holy Place) and establish the Kingdom as we mature in the Lord, our soul will work in tandem with our spirit to walk in Kingdom principles. Where the spirit and soul go, the flesh will follow. Our thoughts, words, and deeds come in line with the Word of God, and Hell will begin to tremble at the restoration of Christ's image in our being. This has been God's plan from the very beginning. We see this dynamic of a renewed mind and cleansed soul linked to learning and following His commandments.

Now it shall come to pass, if you diligently obey the voice of the LORD your God, to observe carefully all His commandments which I command you today, that the LORD your God will set you high above all nations of the earth. And all these blessings shall come upon you and overtake you, because you obey the voice of the LORD your God: (Deuteronomy 28:1–2)

Be strong and of good courage, for to this people you shall divide as an inheritance the land which I swore to their fathers to give them. Only be strong and very courageous, that you may observe to do according to all the law which Moses My servant commanded you; do not turn from it to the right hand or to the left, that you may prosper wherever you go. This Book of the Law shall not depart from your mouth, but you shall meditate in it day and night, that you may observe to do according to all that is written in it. For then you will make your way prosperous, and then you will have good success. Have I not commanded you? Be strong and of good courage; do not be afraid, nor be dismayed, for the LORD your God is with you wherever you go. (Joshua 1:6–9)

But his delight is in the law of the LORD, and in His law he meditates day and night. He shall be like a tree planted by the rivers of water, that brings forth its fruit in its season, whose leaf also shall not wither; and whatever he does shall prosper. (Psalm 1:2–3)

I chose these three sets of verses in sequence to show a pattern. In Judaism, the First (or Old) Testament is not referred to as the Old Testament: it is called the Tanakh. The Tanakh is broken down into three sections: the Torah, the Nevi'im (Prophets), and the Ketuvim (the Writings). First, the Torah established the ways of God for His people; the LORD clearly defined both sinful and righteous acts. The very first book of the Prophets that became part of the Bible was Joshua. Immediately, the words in that book point back to the commandments of God and connect them to things going well in our lives. Now, we get the first book of the Writings, which is the Psalms, and it points back to a righteous man who will delight and meditate on the commandments of God. Finally, we get to Jesus. He had real problems with the rabbis replacing God's commandments with their own, as we see in His words:

…making the word of God of no effect through your tradition which you have handed down. And many such things you do. (Mark 7:13)

And, finally, Jesus declared:

If you love Me, keep My commandments. (John 14:15)

If you keep My commandments, you will abide in My love, just as I have kept My Father's commandments and abide in His love. (John 15:10)

The Holy Spirit indwells believers to lead us into all truth (John 16:13). He becomes a spiritual force to help us establish new behaviors rather than abiding by what our hellish taskmasters taught us in the past. He is here to lead us into steps of freedom, wholeness, and blessing. We purposefully work with the Holy Spirit to establish new Kingdom behaviors. We carry out these behaviors on purpose, regardless of how our flesh feels. We then bring the family environment in line with the Kingdom. We begin teaching God's ways to our children through our words and actions. Doing things God's way becomes the family's way of doing things. Over time, God's instruction replace whatever lessons we learned from Hell's Torah. Whatever genetic alterations have been made through sinful behavior will be replaced by Heaven's reinstituting the image of God within our DNA and being. In every situation, obedience to the Word of God (especially when it isn't easy) is an act of spiritual warfare!

For those who take this seriously, the Word declares:

Therefore know that the LORD your God, He is God, the faithful God who keeps covenant and mercy for a thousand generations with those who love Him and keep His commandments. (Deuteronomy 7:9)

What a powerful statement. While the encoding (and cursing) from the Iniquity Force can only flow through three or four generations, the Kingdom of God can flow to a thousand generations. This fight is more than just about life and making it better. We are fighting for ourselves and future generations of our bloodline! We are fighting for our children, our children's children, etc. At this realization, our warfare moves from an act about self to a selfless act for others. Selflessness is the way of the Kingdom.

Moving Forward and Counteracting the Enemy's Moves

The Holy Spirit must lead the process of sanctification. We must start with a spiritual force that prompts new behavior for it to work. As we prayerfully study the Word of God, the Holy Spirit will show us an incorrect thought pattern to begin working on. The Holy Spirit will never lead us where His power cannot lead us to victory. I also need to point out that the Holy Spirit will only have us face one "giant" (if you will) at a time. The Holy Spirit is gentle and graceful as He works in our lives. He always convicts but never condemns. He also never overwhelms. One of the enemy's tactics is that if he cannot stop us from attacking an internal giant, he will try to overwhelm us by revealing dozens of them at once. The Holy Spirit will never do such a thing. Instead, He will empower us to address one, drive it out, and replace the enemy's lies with Kingdom truths. Once we have established that correction, He will move us on to the next issue to be addressed. Like in warfare in the physical world, we cannot fight wars on multiple fronts.

There are several steps to taking down the giants within:

1. Repent
2. Declare war
3. Learn God's Word (through study and meditation)
4. Engage in warfare
5. Build a new, fortified area for God

Now that we have outlined these steps, let's examine each one in detail.

1. Repent. Everything starts with repentance.

From that time Jesus began to preach and to say, "Repent, for the kingdom of heaven is at hand." (Matthew 4:17)

This wasn't a one-time message from our Messiah. It was His central message everywhere He went! Whether we are first coming into the Kingdom or advancing in the Kingdom, everything begins with repentance.

As I detailed in my book, *The Sheeriyth Imperative*, sin empowers the enemy. The moment we repent of sin and are covered by the blood of Jesus, the enemy loses power in that area! It removes the enemy's power source and his legal right to operate!

We must repent of responding incorrectly to whatever doorway event gave entrance to the enemy. We need to repent of believing the lie the enemy enforced. We need to repent of every time we reacted to life through the lie planted by the enemy. If we spend time before the Lord and give the Holy Spirit time to work, He may remind us of events in our lives that either need repentance or forgive others. It helps to keep a journal and work through repenting and forgiving, until we are ready to declare war in that area.

2. Declare war. In declaring war, we begin calling out the lies of the enemy. We announce before Heaven and Hell that what the taskmasters of Hell have taught us were nothing more than lies and deception. We declare that we will not live life under the yoke of the enemy. We will not view life through a distorted lens or respond to life through tainted instructions. We choose to no longer be those people anymore. We choose to be like Jesus! It is also important to declare that the spirit behind this action or belief no longer has a legal right to be there, and we can then command it to leave, in Jesus' name. This may take more than one time to accomplish. Remember, we are driving the enemy out of our souls and our lives. We must show this worker from Hell no mercy and give it no quarter.

3. Learn God's Word. In referring to learning God's Word, I'm not talking about general reading of the Word. I am talking about targeted study. Whatever area we want to overcome, we can research verses addressing that subject—not just in general, but about how we react and respond in those situations. It's important that we make sure there is a "doing" element to what you're researching. James warns us of just "knowing" the Word without "doing" it:

> So then, my beloved brethren, let every man be swift to hear, slow to speak, slow to wrath; for the wrath of man does not produce the righteousness of God. Therefore lay aside all filthiness and overflow of wickedness, and receive with meekness the implanted word, which is able to save your souls. But be doers of the word, and not hearers only, deceiving yourselves. For if anyone is a hearer of the word and not a doer, he is like a man observing his natural face in a mirror; for he observes himself, goes away, and immediately forgets what kind of man he was. But he who looks into the perfect law of liberty and continues in it, and is not a forgetful hearer but a doer of the work, this one will be blessed in what he does. (James 1:19–25)

For those established in the Greco-Roman mindset, learning the truth is not enough. We can brag about it and impress friends and neighbors with our depth of understanding. However, biblically and Hebraically, we do not really "know" that truth. Only "doers" know. Until we can "do" the Word, we can never really know the depths of its power.

As recorded repeatedly in the Torah, the children of Israel responded to the commandments of God with the phrase "we will hear, and we will do." In the original Hebrew, there are several occurrences of this phrase in which the response is reversed: "we will do, and we will hear." This reversal in the phrase troubled the sages of Israel for quite some time. Eventually, they realized that the only way you can really "hear" what

God meant was through the experience of obedience. God's ways are not our ways (Isaiah 55:89). They may seem foreign to our carnal nature, and we cannot see the logic in God's instruction. Hindsight always has 20/20 vision. Only after experiencing the blessing of obedience can we understand God's wisdom. The prophet Samuel reminded the erring King Saul that "obedience is better than sacrifice" (1 Samuel 15:22). I would add that obedience to God can be a sacrifice as well. We must sacrifice our carnal response to a situation by intentionally responding through the instruction of God, even if our flesh is screaming the entire time. Remember, this whole endeavor is warfare with the enemy and our carnal nature.

I always keep a notebook with my Bible to write down Scriptures I want to memorize and use in warfare, whether internal or external. Not only do I write down the verses, but I include a short note as to why they are important. Over the years, I've heard from many who use 3 x 5 note cards to help them with this process. No matter what study methods we choose, it's critical that we take the time to memorize the Scripture and establish it in our hearts.

Since we're dealing with something we "do," it's also important to begin seeing ourselves in situations involving the topic we're studying and then rehearsing ways we might respond biblically. This is not guided visualization in which some spirit guides what us internally see in our minds. Instead, this is simply thinking about how it would look—personally—to respond according to God's Word.

I surrendered to ministry on my thirteenth birthday. I had previously resisted the call of God on my life for over a year, because I hated getting up in public to read or give an oral report. In fact, in those situations, I stuttered badly. I would gladly have taken an *F* for an assignment rather than attempt to get up and humiliate myself before the class. So it didn't seem possible that God was asking me to serve Him in this way. However, I did answer His call, and the pastor assigned me to speak to our congregation the following week.

"Are you crazy?!" I thought! "I haven't even been trained yet," I told him. But he insisted, and God used the sermon's theme—the end times—to finally motivate me to say "yes." I worked on the presentation the entire week, making pages of notes. I was ready to let the congregants have it! Although I didn't stutter, I spoke so fast that I sounded like a chipmunk from the cartoons. I shared every word from my ten pages of notes (which could have easily produced a twenty-five-minute message) in about five minutes. The entire time, my knees trembled, and I was sweating through my shirt. Afterward, my pastor commented that he should have recorded the message. That way, he could have slowed down the tape to hear what I said.

This event troubled me more than anything else I had experienced in my young life. How could I fulfill God's calling when I would crash and burn like that I did that day? I spent a lot of time spent in tears and prayer, believing I had failed God.

But then…the Holy Spirit took over. He began to show me a vision of speaking before large audiences with confidence. Every time I prayed about serving in the ministry (which was often in those days), He showed me the same thing. Eventually, what He showed me got deep into my heart. Today, I am more comfortable standing before thousands than I am in one-on-one conversations. In retrospect, I realize the Spirit of God was showing me the future. Over the years, I've had the honor of proclaiming God's Word at conferences with as many as three thousand-plus attendees, and in front of congregations in sanctuaries that could seat ten thousand. Once the correct behavior got into my heart, the rest of me followed.

World-class athletes around the world use the same technique. They visualize the perfect move, the fastest run, etc., until it becomes a part of them. I first heard of this from a soldier who found himself as a prisoner of war in Vietnam. He loved playing golf. In the confinement of a prison camp, he would envision himself playing on his favorite golf course to keep his sanity. Since he spent years in confinement, he eventually got bored and developed more challenging golf courses in his mind. He mentally "played them" repeatedly. Once he was released and returned home, he was surprised to discover that his golf game had improved drastically. His body followed what he had developed in his mind.

The enemy uses this concept as well. How many people see themselves in defeat and constantly rerun those defeats in their minds? How many have mentally yielded to temptation before ever actually carrying out the act in real life? Is this what the Apostle Paul would have termed as "a vain imagination?"

Meditating on the Word is more than just repeating it a thousand times. We turn over the Scripture to look at it from different angles, asking questions such as: What did God mean by this instruction? How is it carried out in real life? How would it look if I responded the way God says to respond? This is all part of the biblical process of meditating on the Word.

4. Engage in warfare. Dynamic warfare involves more than just praying against the enemy (although that is important). Since we are tripartite beings (having a mind, body, and soul), we must operate with a threefold response. We must think, speak, and act according to the Word of God in every situation. We must bring our minds and emotions into subjection to Christ and His teachings to properly engage the enemy. When we do, our faith can soar. It is like upgrading from a BB gun to a .308 Winchester rifle. The Spirit of God can move through our thoughts, words, and actions and allow the anointing and authority of the Messiah to flow. Why? Because our thoughts, words, and actions are in line with what Jesus would have done. God's power will only flow where the character of Christ has been established. The character of Christ and the Word are always the same. Remember, Jesus is the Word made flesh.

In every situation, we should purposefully respond to life, "doing" the Word on purpose. Imagine for a moment the work soldiers invest in taking care of their weapons. With great care, they will strip down a weapon and meticulously inspect, clean, and lubricate all its parts. If any part is worn or cracked, they will replace the part (or find an armorer who will). They then reassemble the weapon and conduct dry-fire testing to ensure everything is in order. If they properly develop expertise in the use of weapons and properly maintain them, they will serve the soldiers well in the heat of battle. For dedicated warriors, weapons become an extension of who they are.

Our thoughts, words, and actions are a part of who we are. Are you bringing yours into submission to God, and are they such that the Holy Spirit can place His anointing upon them? Or are you allowing the enemy to sabotage your weapons of warfare? Are the communications down with headquarters (Heaven)? Do your weapons misfire, or worse, are those around you victims of friendly fire? These are questions we need to ask ourselves with stark honesty. Until we assess where we are, we can never make the right adjustments (or repairs) to get to where we need to be.

5. Build a new, fortified area for God. Once we have won an area for the Kingdom, we must establish a perimeter around it. We must guard this area and complete further fortifications of it. The enemy will always seek territory in our lives that he once inhabited. Jesus provided a stern warning related to this in His teachings on deliverance:

> When an unclean spirit goes out of a man, he goes through dry places, seeking rest, and finds none. Then he says, "I will return to my house from which I came." And when he comes, he finds it empty, swept, and put in order. Then he goes and takes with him seven other spirits more wicked than himself, and they enter and dwell there; and the last state of that man is worse than the first. So shall it also be with this wicked generation. (Matthew 12:43–45)

We cannot leave the areas we've conquered empty and open. We must continue reinforcing God's Word in our minds and lives. We must always stand on guard and be vigilant, always watching for the enemy to encroach on his old areas of operation. We must labor to stay filled with the Word and with the Spirit of God. God calls us to be ever on guard over our thoughts and emotions. If something gets out of line, we have the weapons and authority to capture and bring them into submission to Christ and the Word.

Prayer

Father, I come before you in Jesus' name. I know the enemy has built strongholds within my soul to keep me from serving you properly. I invite the Holy Spirit to invade my soul and to help me target these strongholds, destroy them, and drive out the tacit influence of the enemy. My heart's cry is to be led by your Spirit and your Word alone. I commit this day to use the weapons of my warfare to bring every thought into captivity to Christ. I will renew my mind according to your Word and will live out the teachings of your Word purposefully on earth.

I bind the gatekeepers and watchers within these strongholds. I declare they will no longer influence me. In Jesus' name, I mark their fortified areas within my soul for destruction. I will not respond to them or listen to them. I repent of whatever sin or situation that gave them a place in my life. I choose to forgive anyone they used to wound me in order to gain access to me. I cover any strongholds in the blood of Jesus. I declare that I am led by the Holy Spirit alone. I choose to walk in the Spirit and not in the flesh.

Father, I stand on your Word that you will cause me both to want to follow your ways and then to do that—to please you (Philippians 2:13). I will live for Jesus and honor His kingship in my life with every thought, word, and action. I look to your Spirit to assist me in this warfare for my soul, in Jesus' name.

Review Questions

1. Are behavioral tendencies genetic, environmental, or both?
2. What three steps are used by the enemy to establish iniquity within an individual?
3. By the time a children reach the age of five, they have learned _____ percent to _____ percent of everything they will ever learn.
4. What three sources can our thoughts, feelings, and actions come from?
5. What is the correlation between the Second Heaven and the soul?
6. What spiritual truth is revealed in two of the Greek words Paul uses for "redemption"?
7. What happens to our souls when we are born again?
8. How long does it take to rewire the brain with new thought patterns and habits?
9. The enemy always brings chaos and unreality. How does Almighty God reestablish His reality both on the earth and in individuals?
10. How can we be sure we know the Word (i.e., the commandments of God)?
11. What five steps are necessary to bring down strongholds and conquer our giants within?

THE POWER OF IDEAS AND SOCIETY

> ...that we should no longer be children, tossed to and fro and carried about with every wind of doctrine, by the trickery of men, in the cunning craftiness of deceitful plotting,
>
> EPHESIANS 4:14

Our study has already established that the Hebraic concept of doctrine (or doctrines) is instructions on how to live. Again, the Greek word used for "doctrine" is *didaskalia* (did-as-kal-ee'-ah), which means "teaching, instruction, and precepts."[66] What is most interesting is how the Apostle Paul describes these doctrines as coming from "every wind." The Holy Spirit is not the only One who moves as a wind in the earth; so does the tacit influence of principalities, powers, and rulers of darkness. In *The Kingdom Priesthood*, I outlined the biblical truth regarding the principality wars and how they have governed all nations since the Tower of Babel. What we will discover in this chapter is that not only individuals can have strongholds, but so can cultures, segments of society, and even nations.

> But even if our gospel is veiled, it is veiled to those who are perishing, whose minds the god of this age has blinded, who do not believe, lest the light of the gospel of the glory of Christ, who is the image of God, should shine on them. (2 Corinthians 4:3–4)

Over the years, I've pondered the truths of 2 Corinthians 4:3—4, in which the Apostle Paul states that the god of this age and (of course) his agents of darkness never cease in their labors to blind the minds of men to keep them from the truth of the Gospel. How does this blinding occur? The fallen immortals breathe across cultures and nations through the winds of doctrine.

Where Do Ideas Come From?

Ideas can be dropped into our souls seemingly out of nowhere. When this happens, we call it inspiration. These ideas are like living things. Sometimes they grow, and sometimes they die in the mind—unrealized. Ideas can transform lives and society. These ideas can transport a culture into a golden age of prosperity or bring about such moral decay that it destroys itself. Unfortunately, immature believers can still be subject to the winds of doctrines, empowered by the power of darkness, that sweep through the channels of society.

Ideas can originate from three places:

1. An individual's creativity
2. The Spirit of God
3. The fallen spirits of darkness

In this chapter, we will examine fallen spirits' influences on society. The ideas that these ancient spirits whisper into the minds of people can serve as seeds of change. As the ideas grow and spread to others, they soon become a foothold. Eventually, those footholds become strongholds. These strongholds of the enemy shade our perception of the world around us. Denizens of these strongholds work in concert with their counterparts on the outside to reinforce the lies they've convinced us are accurate. These strongholds not only speak *to* us, but unfortunately, they speak *through* us to those around us. (Just watch the evening propaganda masquerading as news reports.) For unregenerate souls (and believers still in bondage), we become active agents in spreading these lies within our families and communities.

The more individuals infected with these doctrines of demons, the more momentum and spiritual power they generate. These hellish ideas resonate with the carnal nature of lost humanity. At that moment, these dark ideas take on the form of a mind virus. Most of the time, they produce negative emotions to fuel their transmission throughout society. Anger and rage seem to be the emotions of choice, although they can also flourish greatly through greed and lust.

> Do not love the world or the things in the world. If anyone loves the world, the love of the Father is not in him. For all that is in the world—the lust of the flesh, the lust of the eyes, and the pride of life—is not of the Father but is of the world. And the world is passing away, and the lust of it; but he who does the will of God abides forever. (1 John 2:15–17)

The Apostle John warned us about the carriers of Hell's mind viruses. Most of the time, we quickly read over them in 1 John 2:15–17, but we never take the time to biblically define "the lust of the flesh, the lust of the eyes, and the pride of life." Let's take a few moments to examine each of these weapons of the enemy.

In the *Annotated Reference Bible,* author Finis Dake takes the time to define what the Apostle John is referring to biblically. I have compiled his notes into a fluid outline for our use.

Three Classes of Things in the World System[67]

I. **The Lust of the Flesh**
    Seventeen Works of the Flesh
    1) **Adultery.** Greek: *moicheia* (GSN-<G3430>), unlawful sexual relations between men and women, single or

married (Matthew 15:19; Mark. 7:21; John. 8:3;
Galatians 5:19). Note the related Greek: verbs, *moichao*
(GSN-<G3429>) (Matthew. 5:32, notes; 19:9; Mark
10:11–12), and *moicheuo* (GSN-<G3431>) (Matthew.
5:27–28; 19:18; Mark 10:19; Luke 16:18; 18:20; John
8:4; Romans 2:22; 13:9; James 2:11; Revelation 2:22).

2) **Fornication.** Greek: *porneia* (GSN-<G4202>), same as
adultery above besides all manner of other unlawful relations (notes, Mt. 5:32).

3) **Uncleanness.** Greek: *akatharsia* (GSN-<G167>), whatever is opposite of purity; including sodomy, homosexuality, lesbianism, pederasty, bestiality, and all other forms
of sexual perversion (Galatians 5:19; Matthew 23:27;
Romans 1:21–32; 6:19; 2 Corinthians 12:21; Ephesians
4:19; 5:3; Colossians 3:5; 1 Thessalonians 2:3; 4:7; 2
Peter 2; Jude).

4) **Lasciviousness.** Greek: *aselgeia* (GSN-<G766>), licen-
tiousness, lustfulness, unchastity, and lewdness. Translated "lasciviousness" (Mark. 7:22; 2 Corinthians 12:21;
Galatians 5:19; Ephesians 4:19; 1 Peter 4:3; Jude 1:4);
"wantonness" (Romans 13:13; 2 Peter 2:18); and "filthy"
(2 Peter 2:7). Lasciviousness is promoting or partaking
of that which tends to produce lewd emotions; anything
tending to foster sex sin and lust. That is why many
worldly pleasures have to be avoided by Christians—so
that lasciviousness may not be committed.

5) **Idolatry.** Greek: *eidololatreia* (GSN-<G1495>), image-
worship (1 Corinthians 10:14; Galatians 5:20; Colossians
3:5; 1 Peter 4:3). Idolatry includes anything on which
affections are passionately set; extravagant admiration of
the heart (Ephesians 5:5; Colossians 3:5).

6) **Witchcraft.** Greek: *pharmakeia* (GSN-<G5331>), sorcery, the practice of dealing with evil spirits; magical

incantations and casting spells and charms upon one by means of drugs and potions of various kinds (Galatians 5:20; Revelation 9:21; 18:23; cp. Revelation 21:8; 22:15. See note b, Luke 12:29). Enchantments were used to inflict evil, pains, hatred, sufferings, and death, or to bring good, health, love and other blessings.

7) **Hatred.** Greek: *echthra* (GSN-<G2189>), enmity (Luke. 23:12; Romans 8:7; Ephesians 2:15–16; James 4:4); hatred (Galatians 5:20). Bitter dislike, abhorrance, malice and ill will against anyone; tendency to hold grudges against or be angry at someone.

8) **Variance.** Greek: *eris* (GSN-<G2054>), note, Rom. 1:29. Dissensions, discord, quarreling, debating; and disputes.

9) **Emulations.** Greek: *zeloi* (GSN-<G2205>), envies, jealousies; striving to excel at the expense of another; seeking to surpass and outdo others; uncurbed rivalry spirit in religion, business, society, and other fields of endeavor. Translated "zeal" (John 2:17; Romans 10:2; 2 Corinthians 7:11; 9:2; Philippians 3:6; Colossians 4:13); "fervent mind" (2 Corinthians 7:7); "envy" (Acts 13:45; Romans 13:13; 1 Corinthians 3:3; 2 Corinthians 12:20; James 3:14–15); "jealousy" (2 Corinthians 11:2); "indignation" (Acts 5:17; Hebrews 10:27); and "emulation" (Galatians 5:20).

10) **Wrath.** Greek: *thumos* (GSN-<G2372>), "wrath" (Galatians 5:20; Luke 4:28; Acts 19:28; 2 Corinthians 12:20; Ephesians 4:31; Colossians 3:8; Hebrews 11:27; Revelation 12:12; 14:8, 10, 19; 15:1, 7; 16:1; 18:3); "indignation" (Romans 2:8); and "fierceness" (Revelation 16:19; 19:15). Turbulent passions; domestic and civil turmoil; rage; determined and lasting anger.

11) **Strife.** Greek: *eritheia* (GSN-<G2052>), "strife" (Gal. 5:20; 2Cor. 12:20; Php. 2:3; Jas. 3:14,16); "contention"

(Php. 1:16; Rom. 2:8). Disputations; jangling; strife about words; angry contentions; contest for superiority or advantage; strenuous endeavor to equal or pay back in kind the wrongs done to one.

12) **Seditions.** Greek: *dichostasia* (GSN-<G1370>), "divisions" (Romans 16:17; 1 Corinthians 3:3); "seditions, parties, and factions" (Galatians 5:20). Popular disorder; stirring up strife in religion, government, home, or any other place.

13) **Heresies** (note, Acts 5:17).

14) **Envyings.** Greek: *phthonoi* (GSN-<G5355>) (Galatians 5:21; Matthew 27:18; Mark 15:10; Romans 1:29; Philippians 1:15; 1 Timothy 6:4; Titus 3:3; James 4:5; 1 Peter 2:1). Pain, ill will, and jealousy at the good fortune or blessings of another; the basest of all degrading and disgraceful passions.

15) **Murders.** Greek: *phonoi* (GSN-<G5408>) (note, Matthew 15:18) to kill; to spoil or mar the happiness of another; hatred (1 John 3:15).

16) **Drunkeness.** Greek: *methai* (GSN-<G3178>) (Galatians 5:21; Luke 21:34; Romans 13:13). Living intoxicated; a slave to drink; drinking bouts.

17) **Revelings.** Greek: *komoi* (GSN-<G2970>) (Galatians 5:21; 1 Peter 4:3); rioting (Romans 13:13). Lascivious and boisterous feastings with obscene music and other sinful activities; pleasures; carousings.[68]

II. **The Lust of the Eyes:**
1) **Lust for women** (Matthew 5:28; Job 31:1)
2) **Eyes full of adultery**—even men with men and women with women (2 Peter 2:14; Romans 1:18–28)
3) **Covetousness** (Psalm 10:8; Luke 12:15)
4) **All things desired** (Ecclesiastes 2:10)

5) **Idolatry** (Ezekiel 6:9; 18:6–15)
6) **All kinds of evil** (Matthew 6:23; 7:22)

III. The Pride of Life:

1) **Self-righteousness** (Job 32:1)
2) **Positions** (Genesis 3:5; Ezekiel 28:11–17; 1 Timothy 3:6; 3 John 1:9)
3) **Power** (Leviticus 26:19)
4) **Riches** (Psalm 39:6; Ezekiel 28:5)
5) **Beauty** (Ezekiel 28:11, 17)
6) **Strength to war** (2 Chronicles 26:16)
7) **Constant boasting of one's self;** glorying in sexual activity; pleasures; and all the vanity of life (1 John 2:15; Psalms 24:4; 36:2; Isaiah 3:16)[69]

In three short statements for the faithful Berean, the Apostle John provides the leading carriers that principalities, powers, and rulers of darkness use for their mind viruses. Any mind virus of the enemy will ride on one of these aspects to infect uninoculated individuals with their lies. (Inoculation comes through salvation and renewing one's mind according to the Word of God.)

In my past books, I have dealt with three mind viruses that the priesthood of darkness implanted into the minds of men and women in the nineteenth century. These hellish concepts were:

✢ Evolution
✢ Eugenics
✢ Spiritism

These three mind viruses took over science and significant portions of Christianity alike. Scientists began rejecting the biblical account of Creation in exchange for the fable that says humanity descended from apes. At the same time, many congregations began to dabble in the

occult by holding séances in the basements of their churches. The Holy
Spirit quickly began to be replaced with demonic spirits weaving their
lies to replace the Gospel of the Kingdom. Humanity and the Church
alike are suffering to this day from these three mind viruses. This triple
threat of occult philosophies combined into a hellish storm of satanic
perfection in Nazi Germany.

Today, we are witnessing the fruit of a fourth mind virus that infected
Nazi Germany and continues ravaging cultures and societies worldwide.
One of the more recent fruits of this mind virus is the "woke" movement.
Those infected with the "woke" mind virus are immune to established
science, facts, logic, and even history. As heavily caffeinated zombies,
they prefer to infect any source of truth and twist it to match their distorted reality. The question needs to be asked, "What is the taproot of
this mind-warping plant that also infected the Nazi party in Germany?"
The Nazis were a socialist party.

While in previous books I've dealt with how the first three concepts
were used by Hell to forge the belief systems of the Nazis, I have yet
to deal with the fourth mind virus. We need to understand this fourth
concept, because it affects our nation and the Church within Western
society. This concept is communism. Various shades of dark gray always
transport those caught in its web into communism: they are progressivism and socialism. The Nazi Party in Germany was a socialist movement. Progressivism, socialism, and communism all spring from the
same toxic taproot.

Here are some famous quotes regarding socialism and communism.

❖ "Socialism is the same as communism, only better English."
—George Bernard Shaw[70]
❖ "The goal of socialism is communism." —Vladimir Lenin[71]
❖ "All socialism involves slavery." —Herbert Spencer[72]

Karl Marx was not the originator of communism. Instead, he pla-
giarized the concept and gave it a name. This concept originated in AD

1666 and flowed from a false Jewish messiah who was an adept in Kabbalistic magic. His name was Shabbatai Zevi.

Robert Sepehr, an author, producer, and anthropologist specializing
in linguistics, archeology, and paleobiology, makes the following obser-
vations regarding Zevi:

1. In 1666, an exceptionally charismatic Rabbi and Kabbalist
    by the name of Sabbatai Zevi (1626–1676) declared
    himself to be the Messiah. Born to an affluent family in
    Western Anatolia, he was a particularly eccentric mystic
    who had attained a massive following of over one million
    devotees during his lifetime, roughly half of the world's
    Jewish population in the 17th century.[73]

2. But what are these "holy sparks" and where did they come
    from? Isaac Luria, whose interpretation of the Kabbalah
    is now most widely used and accepted, explained that
    God created the world by forming 10 vessels to hold the
    "Divine Light". God intended this original Light to radiate
    out, fill the world and illuminate everything around us.
    But as God poured the Light into the vessels, the Divine
    Light was so powerful that the vessels couldn't contain it.
    With a huge explosion, the vessels shattered, and sparks
    of this Divine Light became embedded into the world of
    matter. (5, 11) The material world had trapped these sparks
    of Divine Light; God's presence was hidden and unable
    to shine forth. It then became the task for us (presumably
    the chosen ones) to free these holy sparks. The manner in
    which people approached and interacted with the material
    universe could set these sparks free and repair the world.[74]

3. This process is called "repairing the world", and it involves
    all of one's actions: how one treats fellow human beings,
    works, plays, thinks, and interacts with all aspects of the
    environment at any given moment in time. Therefore,

these "heretical" Kabbalists believed that acts that benefit
God included deliberate forays into the world of sin, where
the illusory nature of evil could be more readily exposed,
and the sparks thereby elevated to their Source.[75]

In other words, salvation can be achieved through entering all aspects
of sin to free the divine sparks: salvation through the works of sin. Shabbatai would have fit well into the modern Church. Here is one of the
blessings he developed for the feasts:

Baruch atah Adonai, Elohainu Melech ha-olam; matir issurim:

Blessed art thou, Lord our God, King of the Universe,
who makes the forbidden things permissible.[76]

Through a revolution of values, what was formerly sacred became
profane, and what was formerly profane had become sacred.[77]

Shabbatai's rise to fame was cut short after prophesying that Israel
would become a nation again while residing in a Muslim nation. The
sheik was happy about the wealth brought into his region by the Jewish
pilgrims (large portions of Judaism at that time believed he was the Messiah). However, after Shabbatai's announcement regarding the future
return of Israel, he was given the choice between converting to Islam or
being put to death through beheading.

Years later, another Jew would pick up Shabbatai's mantle and
accomplish what he could not. This man's name was Jacob Frank. Jacob
Frank, born fifty years after the death of Shabbatai Zevi, proclaimed
he was the incarnation of Shabbatai at the age of twenty-five and that
he was the living messiah for all Jews. Frank also announced he would
complete what his predecessor could not (because he was weak). Four
years later, Frank formed an official body of believers in the Kabbalah,
which became known as Zoharist. Their most sacred writing was the
Zohar, which became the most important writing among the 550 books

that make up the teachings of Kabbalah. Anyone who studies the Zohar is reading the instructions of Jacob Frank. Jacob Frank became a nihilist in his thinking and pushed this philosophy to its limits.

Gershom Scholem, a noted Jewish scholar and university professor, has made the following comments regarding Frank:

> If the full truth be told, however, even after one has taken into account Frank's unscrupulous opportunism, his calculated deceits, and his personal ambitions, none of which really concerns us here, **he remains a figure of tremendous satanic power.**[78] (Emphasis added)

Frank was a nihilist, and his nihilism possessed a rare authenticity. Certainly, its primitive ferocity is frightening to behold.[79]

Regarding Frank's theology, Scholem comments:

> **Hence, it is necessary to cast off the domination of these laws, which are laws of death and harmful to mankind.** To bring this about, the Good God has sent messengers such as the patriarchs "who dug wells," Moses, Jesus, and others, into the world. **Moses pointed out the true way, but it was found to be too difficult, whereupon he resorted to "another religion" and presented men with "the Law of Moses," whose commandments are injurious and useless.** "The Law of the Lord," on the other hand—the spiritual Torah of the Sabbatians—"is perfect" (Ps. 19:8), only no man has yet been able to attain it.[80] (Emphasis added)

> From the abyss, if only the "burden of silence" is borne, "holy knowledge" will emerge. The task, then, is "to acquire knowledge," "and the passageway to knowledge is to combine with the nations" but not, of course, to intermingle with them. He who reaches the destination will lead a life of anarchic liberty as

a free man. "The place that we are going to tolerates no laws, for all that comes from the side of Death, whereas we are bound for Life." **The name of this place is "Edom" or "Esau," and the way to it, which must be followed by the light of "knowledge" (gnosis) and under the "burden of silence" through the depths of the abyss, is called "the way to Esau."**[81] (Emphasis added)

Why is Jacob Frank so important? He teamed up with two other men to form a notorious organization. These men were Mayer Amschel Rothschild and Adam Weishaupt. Frank was a founding member of the Illuminati! He helped develop the five goals of Illuminism:

1. Abolition of monarchies and all ordered governments.
2. Abolition of private property and inheritances.
3. Abolition of patriotism and nationalism.
4. Abolition of family life and the institution of marriage, and the establishment of communal education of children.
5. Abolition of all religion.[82]

While history claims the Illuminati was destroyed centuries ago, why are we seeing these goals being carried out in the Western world today? Frank is also the true father of what Karl Marx termed "communism." Here is a short list of historical figures who were Jacob Frank's devotees.

- Moses Hess
- Karl Marx
- Friedrich Engels
- Theodore Herzl
- Vladimir Lenin
- Joseph Stalin
- Benito Mussolini
- Moa Tse-tung
- Pol Pot

✤ Fidel Castro
✤ Adolf Hitler

Communism is the modern version of Illuminism. It is the promise of Utopia without God, a Millennial Reign without Christ. But, this Utopia is built on the dead bodies of all who resist.

✤ **French Revolution (the Testing Grounds)** – More than fifty thousand people died in this terror-filled revolution.
✤ **Soviet Union** – More than twenty-six million of its own citizens were killed for the promise of a Utopia.
✤ **Moa and Communist China** – More than fifty million of its own citizens were killed for the promise of a Utopia.
✤ **Mussolini** – More than 430,000 were killed under his reign of terror for a promised Utopia.
✤ **Pol Pot** – More than two million died in his killing fields for a promised Utopia.
✤ **Fidel Castro** – More than twenty thousand were killed for the promise of a Utopia.
✤ **America?** – Bill Ayers, former member of the Weather Underground terrorist group, retired professor from the University of Illinois, and friend of President Obama, has estimated that twenty-four million Americans will need to die to produce their promised Utopia.

The first trial run for the Illuminati was the French Revolution, which released two years of absolute horror for the French. Two forces were at play in this revolution: the Frankists and the Jacobins. Both draw their name from Jacob Frank. Jacobinism is alive and well in the United States. If you take the time to Google the term "Jacobin," the top listing is the number-one liberal/leftist magazine in America and not the group that instigated the French Revolution (and attempted to create one in the United States shortly after its founding). This anomaly is because the Jacobins have taken over the Democratic Party and large portions of the Republican Party (RINOs). The Jacobin philosophy has embedded itself into the culture of the Deep State.

The result of the revolution was that France ran into the arms of a dictator—Napoléon Bonaparte. Is this the template the elite will use worldwide to bring such despair that the population will run into the arms of the son of perdition, or Antichrist?

After the French Revolution, the Jacobins set their eyes on Great Britain. But, their attempts to overthrow the British failed horribly. Why? The Jacobin failure can be ultimately attributed to two causes:

1. The great revivals sweeping through Great Britain through English theologian and evangelist John Wesley
2. The intense nationalism of the Scottish people

It would be over a century before Britain and most of Europe would embrace socialism. It took two world wars to accomplish this hellish feat. The purpose of the First World War was to weaken the royal family of Russia, which allowed the communist revolution. There were many purposes for the Second World War. One was to strip Europe of its Protestant belief system and move those nations toward socialism. All these tasks have been accomplished. However, with catalysts of the Third World War appearing on the horizon in our daily news reports, the elite's purposes are becoming clear: to pave the way for the Son of Perdition.

After the Jacobins' failure in Great Britain, they adjusted their strategies. Before a communist revolution could occur in some nations, it was necessary to accomplish two goals first:

1. Destroy nationalism within a nation
2. Weaken the Church within a nation so that it cannot serve as a preserving agent against the infection of Hell's mind virus

It doesn't take a genius to realize that these two obstructions to communism taking over in America have been underway since the turn of the twentieth century. In our day, even Christian authors are warning of the evils of Christian nationalism. While I recognize that nationalism can be taken too far (i.e., to the point of worshipping the state, which is the same goal as that of communism), we need to balance the excesses of nationalism with our task of being salt and light within a nation. Are we going to sit in our churches and allow socialism to take over as the Christians did in Nazi Germany? I refuse to be a part of the "sing a little louder" churches that existed during those dark days. As trains full of Jews (and others) were passing by the churches on Sunday morning, these churchgoers could hear the cries for help from those destined for the gas chambers of the concentration camps. What was their response? They sang their songs a little louder when the trains passed by to drown out the sound of the cries of desperation. May the Church of the Living God never be so spineless again!

We must balance preserving freedom in America without looking to the political arena as a savior for our woes. Since the halls of darkness completely control the political, financial, and most religious circles within society, help is never going to come from them. Our only hope is the fire of God being released in the true Body of Christ and these demonically controlled arenas of our nation to develop once again a healthy fear of the army of Christ and their King!

How Do We Move Forward?

The late Beatles singer/songwriter John Lennon has been credited with saying, "You either transform culture or culture transforms you." When we examine the 1960s, a significant transformation of culture was taking place. While researching the occultist Jack Parsons, I discovered something interesting connected to our topic. In the book, *Sex and Rockets: The Occult World of Jack Parsons*, the author makes the following observation:

> Crowley spoke for this tradition when he said true religion always invokes Dionysus, Aphrodite, and the Muses, which he also called "wine, women, and song." Nowadays we call this magick trinity "Sex and Drugs and Rock 'n' Roll," and celebrate them at Raves that hauntingly resemble the earliest stirrings of cosmic questing by ancestors who dressed in animal skins and looked even more like gorillas than we do.[83]

The revolution of the 1960s was a satanic rave! This so-called magick trinity transformed our culture in America. The youth who participated in this occult work have all grown up; they're now captains of industry, education, finances, and politics. These matured ravers are the forces behind the current satanic rave taking hold of Western society. We are living in the 1960s—version 2.0. Not only are they moving to restore ancient pagan ideology regarding sex, but they're out to redefine the very concept of sexuality. The current woke movement is in lockstep with the five Illuminism principles, and it has grown from Jacob Frank's taproot.

It is essential for the Kingdom warrior not to be moved by the constant waves of the doctrines of demons that flow through culture. Instead, the Kingdom warrior must be firmly anchored to God's truth (reality). The Kingdom of God is the ultimate counterculture. We need to own this fact and stop letting the cultures of darkened humanity change us. We are only effective when we become that "other" culture not subject to the influence of the priesthood of darkness. We must become agents of change in the cultures around us, always pointing to Christ and the Gospel of the Kingdom.

Actually, the Christian TRUTH isn't a religion but a revolution against the kingdom of darkness. —Hans Poley, 1942–1945

There are several things that Kingdom warriors must do:

1. **Examine your belief systems**. Where do the concepts originate from? Do they have their solid origins in the unadulterated Word of God, or can they be traced back to the winds of cultural change?

And do not be conformed to this world, but be transformed by the renewing of your mind, that you may prove what is that good and acceptable and perfect will of God. (Romans 12:2)

2. **Take ownership of walking in the culture of the Kingdom**. The Kingdom of God has its own culture that will flow with the Word and Spirit of God. Never allow yourself to feel embarrassed about walking in the Kingdom. You have the pathway to freedom, healing, and restoration. Be the example and show the world that there is another way.

But sanctify the Lord God in your hearts, and always be ready to give a defense to everyone who asks you a reason for the hope that is in you, with meekness and fear; having a good conscience, that when they defame you as evildoers, those who revile your good conduct in Christ may be ashamed. For it is better, if it is the will of God, to suffer for doing good than for doing evil. (1 Peter 3:15–17)

3. Maintain the fire of God in your life. It is the task of the Kingdom priesthood to seek the fire of God and maintain it. It is the task
of the Kingdom warrior to faithfully carry that fire into the world. We
must fight fire with fire. Only the fire of God can overcome the fire of
Hell!

> And of the angels He says: "Who makes His angels spirits and
> His ministers a flame of fire." (Hebrews 1:7)

Note: While Hebrews 1:7 (and Psalm 104:4, which the writer of
Hebrews quotes) speaks of angels, I believe Kingdom warriors can also
carry God's fire on the earth. We see this on the day of Pentecost. On
the very first Pentecost, Israel gathered around Mount Sinai to witness
the fire of God that was displayed with such power that it frightened
even Moses. On the day of Pentecost, after the Resurrection of the Messiah, tongues of fire fell upon those assembled in the Upper Room. The
120 present there carried that fire into the streets and eventually into
the nations. The book of Acts is still being written today. Will the final
chapters not be like the first? We need God to pour His Spirit upon us
with great power until we are ministers that are a flame of fire for the
Kingdom!

**4. Bind up the power behind the "woke" movement and com-
munism.** Jesus taught on "binding" and "loosing" two times. Although
both teachings have elements of spiritual warfare, only one deals explic-
itly with binding up the power of the enemy. Let's examine each of these
teachings because it's crucial to realize that context is vital for proper
interpretation.

a. Binding and Loosing in Spiritual Warfare

> And I will give you the keys of the kingdom of heaven, and what-
> ever you bind on earth will be bound in heaven, and whatever
> you loose on earth will be loosed in heaven. (Matthew 16:19)

We must properly set the scene to understand Jesus' statement. Jesus had taken His disciples to Mount Hermon, which, historically, has always been connected to the cosmic conflict between Heaven and Hell. On this mount, we have:

✤ The location where the Watchers of Genesis 6 first descended to create a hybrid race known as the Nephilim
✤ The ancient world believed that the cave at this location was the entrance to Hades (gates of Hell)
✤ A grotto to the ancient pagan deity known as Pan (which some connect to Nimrod)
✤ The ancient biblical fortress of Nimrod

Jesus promised that the gates of Hell (the whole council of Hell) would not prevail against those He had called out of Babylon. Yet, in the time of the apostles, the entire council was not there. I documented in *The Shinar Directive* that the leaders among the Watchers of Genesis 6 were still in captivity in New Testament times. They've been slowly released from their captivity since the beginning of the twentieth century, which corresponds with a technological explosion of unprecedented proportions. With this in mind, Jesus spoke to the end-time Church through His disciples in the first century.

It should also be noted that it was on this same mountain that Jesus was transfigured. What a place to show His glory! The Transfiguration of Jesus was an act of spiritual warfare!

Whether or not we realize it, every time we pray for people to be saved, healed, and delivered, we basically bind the power of darkness in their lives and release the Kingdom of God. As the book of Revelation unfolds before us, we may find ourselves in the same situation as young David, the future king of Israel who was facing down a descendant of the Nephilim. The moment David began to say he was in covenant with Almighty God, the giant named Goliath was doomed. On that day, the power of the Kingdom was released from a shepherd's slingshot. The full force of the Kingdom was in that rock hurled at the giant's head. The same power flowed through David's arm as he took the giant's sword and cut off his head. Just hours before, Saul's armor and weapons had proven to be too big for the young shepherd. Now, the sword of a giant fit David's hand perfectly. (David kept that sword and used it throughout his entire life.)

We must become experts in binding and loosing. We have the authority to bind up the power of the enemy and to release the power of the Kingdom of God in every situation. One day, the Remnant will face down giants of their own.

More in the Next Chapter

As we examine the second teaching of Jesus on binding and loosing from Matthew 18:18, it dovetails perfectly into the next chapter regarding the concept of elders in the gates. We will discover that some aspects of spiritual warfare are not so obvious. However, as we will soon find, they are essential to the welfare of our homes, communities, ministries, and nations.

Prayer

Father, help me to examine my heart to ensure that I have not been influenced by the satanic winds of doctrines that have swept through humanity. I repent of any concept, ideology, or even emotion that would align itself with the enemy. I choose the Kingdom and resolve in my heart to walk in the culture of the Kingdom of God alone.

I stand in the authority that has been given to me by King Jesus. I bind up the occult power that is accelerating every aspect of the agenda of the Illuminati in our society. I also release the Kingdom to counter the work of principalities, powers, and the rulers of darkness in the nations. Father, release the fire of God into the hearts of the Remnant worldwide. Let a true revival sweep the planet to reap the final harvest before Jesus returns, in Jesus' name.

Review Questions

1. What are the "winds of doctrines" the Apostle Paul speaks of in Ephesians 4:14?
2. What are the three places from which ideas can originate?
3. What are some of the possible carriers of the satanic winds of doctrine that sweep across cultures?
4. What is a "mind virus"?
5. What was the fourth mind virus that took hold of Nazi Germany?
6. Who was Jacob Frank, and why is he so important in our understanding of modern history?
7. What two goals are the followers of Jacob Frank working on in the Western world?
8. What four steps can the Remnant take to overcome the occult "winds of doctrine" in our time?

8

WATCHMEN AND ELDERS
IN THE GATES

Her husband is known in the gates,
when he sits among the elders of the land.

PROVERBS 31:23

've written, deleted, and started over at least three times as I tackled writing this chapter. My frustration in developing the theme of this chapter doesn't spring from the Word of God; human traditions caused it. From my theological background, I see the fivefold ministry as an ever-present list of five offices that will remain in the Body of Christ until we reach full maturity in the last days. Few believers have researched these offices in their historical context to realize they existed before the establishment of the Church. The Apostle Paul drew from the synagogal model the prophets Ezra and Nehemiah originally established during the Babylonian captivity. Other traditions only recognize pastors, evangelists, and teachers (and missionaries). Some groups add bishops and archbishops to the mix. Finally, it dawned on me to approach this subject differently by using the term "elder." As we will shortly see, the elder has a wide range of biblical applications pertinent to this chapter's topic. It moves beyond those called to ministry to include husbands and wives in their homes.

I chose to start this chapter by quoting from Proverbs 31. During the Friday evening Sabbath meal in every Jewish home worldwide, the husband will read the section of Proverbs 31 regarding the virtuous woman over his wife. Then, he will declare to his children that the Almighty has blessed him to have such a wonderful woman in his life. Part of this blessing includes that he will be known at the gates and sit among the elders of that city or region.

As a child, I would read about the "gates" of a city and think of them as the only gates I had ever seen: small gates in chain-link fences. "Why in the world would someone want to sit there?" I thought when I read this verse of Proverbs. It wasn't until I attended Bible college that I learned the archeological significance of the "elders at the gate." The walls of the ancient cities were a major part of the defensive posture of any town. The larger the city, the more fortified its walls. These walls were so crucial to the well-being of the city that the book of Proverbs warns us:

> Whoever has no rule over his own spirit is like a city broken
> down, without walls. (Proverbs 25:28)

In those days, the fortified walls were so thick that some cities held chariot races on top of them. Chambers located in the wall's immense gates were used by the cities' elders as "offices" where they conducted government and judiciary matters. Within the ancient mindset, these walls and the presence of the elders and judges at the gates were all a vital part of the system to protect those living within the cities. We can add to this dynamic those who were watchmen on the walls and the soldiers who would staff the cities' defensive systems established for protection.

During the Second Temple period, the rabbis borrowed the concept of the elders in the gates of the city and took that mantle upon themselves. The rabbis within a local city would gather to discuss not only theological topics, but even commercial interests, to decide what they would allow or forbid. If the issue or issues were too complex, the group of rabbis would write to the Sanhedrin in Jerusalem for a solution. Gamaliel, the mentor to the Apostle Paul, would consult with other members of the Sanhedrin, come to a consensus, and send back a solution in the form of a letter (or epistle) to that city. (The Church is indebted to Gamaliel. It was at his feet that the young Saul of Tarsus learned to address problems by writing letters. Where would we be without these epistles [letters] of the Apostle Paul?)

Against the cultural backdrop of the rabbis serving as the elders in the gates, Jesus again addressed His disciples regarding "binding" and "loosing."

> Moreover if your brother sins against you, go and tell him his fault between you and him alone. If he hears you, you have gained your brother. But if he will not hear, take with you one or two more, that *by the mouth of two or three witnesses every word may be established.* And if he refuses to hear them, tell it to the church. But if he refuses even to hear the church, let him be to you like a heathen and a tax collector. Assuredly, I say to you, whatever you bind on earth will be bound in heaven, and whatever you loose on earth will be loosed in heaven. Again I say to you that if two of you agree on earth concerning anything that they ask, it will be done for them by My Father in heaven. For where two or three are gathered together in My name, I am there in the midst of them. (Matthew 18:15–20, emphasis added)

When we drop this occurrence of the concept of "binding" and "loosing" into its scriptural context, we discover that Jesus wasn't speaking about supernatural forces, He was speaking of serving as elders at the gates of the Church. Like the elders of old, the elders among the Church would serve as leaders and judiciary members, regarding those called out of spiritual Babylon. Jesus knew the various divisions among the rabbis would seek a foothold in what became known as the Nazarene sect within Judaism. Therefore, Jesus gave authority to His unique community of faith, specifically to those who achieved the spiritual maturity necessary to be considered elders.

The Greek word Jesus used for "church" is *ekklesia* (ek-klay-see'-ah). Jesus has given the leadership of the *ekklesia* authority to make rulings on what they would and would not allow in their faith community. This authority does not fall to those outside the community of faith, including the secular governments administered by principalities, powers, and rulers of darkness. I believe the founding fathers of America understood this dynamic and that's why they included the separation of the civil government from the Church in the First Amendment; it's not separation of church and state, but rather the separation of the state from the Church! Civil government has no business poking its nose into religious affairs. We see the council of the *ekklesia* gathering in Acts 15 to settle a controversy regarding Gentiles coming to faith and being accepted into the Nazarene sect of Judaism at that time in history. In the modern world, we see this concept of "binding" and "loosing" all the time— every time there is a board meeting, whether of a local congregation or an international Christian organization. Unfortunately, we've narrowed the scope of such boards to the business activities of those organizations. I firmly believe we should expand our definition to include spiritual matters. Imagine if councils of elders gathered to pray for the spiritual condition of those under their charge. What if they took the time to bind the spirit of error (1 John 4:6) and loose the Spirit of Truth in their midst? How about binding up the spirit behind "social justice" and the communist "woke" movements? I believe one of the enemy's strategies has been to limit the elders' administration to the mere business of the Church and compel them to relinquish their role over the spiritual condition of their people. The council's ruling in Jerusalem recorded in Acts 15 had spiritual and practical applications. That passage serves as a guide for the *ekkesia* today. (We will expand on this concept a little later in this chapter.)

Levels of Authority

There are times when some of the terms we've inherited from the
Roman Catholic Church cloud spiritual issues. The terms "clergy" and
"laity" could cause us to create artificial separations regarding spiritual
authority and application. The Catholic Church went as far as to claim
that only their clergy had a right to have access to the written Word of
God. During the Reformation, many Protestant believers were tortured
and burned at the stake for having pieces of paper with Scriptures written on them. The Catholic Church was so angry with John Wycliffe for
translating the Word of God into the language of the common people
that it dug up his remains, "tried" him for heresy, and then burned his
bones.

When we examine the biblical standard as outlined in Ephesians
4:11, we discover several essential truths:

And He Himself gave some to be apostles, some prophets, some
evangelists, and some pastors and teachers, for the equipping of
the saints for the work of ministry, for the edifying of the body
of Christ, till we all come to the unity of the faith and of the
knowledge of the Son of God, to a perfect man, to the measure
of the stature of the fullness of Christ. (Ephesians 4:11–13)

God gives the elders the ability to 1) prepare the Body for ministry;
and 2) bring spiritual maturity to all members under their charge, with
Jesus as the standard. This spiritual maturity will result in unity of the
Spirit and in-depth knowledge of the Word.

The priesthood of the believer is universal in the Body of Christ.
Every member has a function and purpose. The elders must watch over
the flock, train them according to their gifts, see them mature into a
deep walk with Almighty God, and move in Kingdom authority.

There are many gates and many elders within the biblical framework of Scripture. The first biblical gate is not the local congregation;

it is the home. It is time to properly establish all the gates and walls of protection for the days ahead.

> Hear, O Israel: The LORD our God, the LORD is one! You shall love the LORD your God with all your heart, with all your soul, and with all your strength. And these words which I command you today shall be in your heart. You shall teach them diligently to your children, and shall talk of them when you sit in your house, when you walk by the way, when you lie down, and when you rise up. You shall bind them as a sign on your hand, and they shall be as frontlets between your eyes. You shall write them on the doorposts of your house and on your gates. (Deuteronomy 6:4–9)

Within the linguistic framework of Deuteronomy 6:4–9, the parents should serve as elders in their homes. Their responsibility is to train their children in the Word of God. Not only are they to teach their children through words, but through actions. Verse 8 speaks of making sure that what the children see and what the parents' hands do align with God's commandments. Then, Moses moves to the topics of the doorposts and gates of each home. Doors and gates provide protection and control regarding who (or what) can and cannot enter. Thus, parents are to serve as gatekeepers or elders in each home. The local pastor cannot do it, nor can any other minister using any other title. The husband and wife are responsible for serving as a team to protect and govern the home.

The Word of God portrays the home as a patriarchal system. However, I must add the caveat that this patriarchal system must be seen through Hebraic eyes, not from the Greco-Roman mindset.

> Adonai, God, said, "It isn't good that the person should be alone. I will make for him a companion suitable for helping him." (Genesis 2:18, CJB)

Eve wasn't created from a bone in Adam's foot so she could be walked on by him. Nor was she created from a bone in his head so she could lord it over him. Eve was created from Adam's side—so she could walk beside him as well as find comfort and protection in his arms. While I believe Scripture makes it clear that the husband should be the leader in the home, that leadership should be carried out within biblical guidelines. Adam couldn't function appropriately without Eve. The first couple was designed to be a team working together.

If the enemy cannot keep us from following the biblical model, he tries his best to push that model out of balance. This imbalance usually happens one of two ways:

1. **The man chooses the path of no accountability by remaining passive and silent.** Adam's silence as recorded in Genesis 3 is deafening. God held Adam accountable for his silence, and the Fall of humanity is known as the sin of Adam. An interesting commandment in the Torah regarding a man and his silence is found in Numbers 30:

> If a woman makes a vow to the LORD, and binds herself by some agreement while in her father's house in her youth, and her father hears her vow and the agreement by which she has bound herself, and her father holds his peace, then all her vows shall stand, and every agreement with which she has bound herself shall stand. But if her father overrules her on the day that he hears, then none of her vows nor her agreements by which she has bound herself shall stand; and the LORD will release her, because her father overruled her. If indeed she takes a husband, while bound by her vows or by a rash utterance from her lips by which she bound herself, and her husband hears it, and makes no response to her on the day that he hears, then her vows shall stand, and her agreements by which she bound herself shall stand. But if her husband overrules her on the day that he hears

it, he shall make void her vow which she took and what she uttered with her lips, by which she bound herself, and the LORD will release her. (Numbers 30:3–8)

Again, this commandment regarding vows speaks to the silence of Adam in the Garden and the fact that Eve had been deceived. This stresses the fact that the man is to serve as an added layer of protection for the woman. In Hebraic thought, women are considered to be "purer" than men. We see this dynamic in the layout of the synagogue during the time of Jesus and the apostles: The men sat toward the front of the synagogue, because they needed the most instruction. The women were seated in an elevated position in the balcony area, because they were considered "purer" than their male counterparts and therefore less in need of the instruction.

When the husband takes on a passive role in the home, it also opens the door for the spirit of Jezebel (a controlling, manipulating, and dominating spirit that is attributed to the biblical character Jezebel) to enter. His silence forces the wife to assume roles God didn't design her for. The resulting woundedness creates a stronghold for Jezebel to enter, dominate, and thrive.

2. **The man chooses the path of a dictatorship and becomes draconian in his position.** His wife is given no say in what goes on in the home. This position is paganistic in its paradigm. In the Greco-Roman world, women were considered substandard. Thanks to the Greek philosophers, the Gentile public thought everything physical was evil and everything spiritual was good. Because women could create life, which was physical, they were considered a necessary evil. The few places where they had any so-called honor was in the pagan temples, where women served as prostitutes and mouthpieces for the gods. Drawing from the fertile soil of our Hebraic heritage, women regained honor and purpose by spreading the Gospel message throughout the Gentile world.

Teamwork Makes the Gates Work

The fear of the LORD is the beginning of knowledge, but fools despise wisdom and instruction. My son, hear the instruction of your father, and do not forsake the law of your mother; for they will be a graceful ornament on your head, and chains about your neck. (Proverbs 1:7–9)

In the traditional Jewish culture of biblical times, the mother was the primary instructor for the first thirteen years of a child's life. It has her duty before God to train the children according to His commandments and teach them how to properly conduct themselves in society. Of course, she was fully supported by her husband in this role as caregiver and instructor. After a son's *bar mitzvah*, the roles would switch. That coming-of-age ritual marked the point when the woman's husband and other men in the community would mentor the teen in the family's chosen field of labor.

Train up a child in the way he should go, and when he is old he will not depart from it. (Proverbs 22:6)

The Jewish community reads this verse with a different perspective than Christians. Christians read it as an instruction to ensure that we raise our children to walk with God. Culturally, this principle was already encoded into every aspect of Jewish society. From a Hebraic mindset, it was the parents' duty to prayerfully consider the vocation each child was gifted—suited—for. First, during the blessing of the children on *Ev Shabbat* (Friday night), the father would lay his hands on each of his children, bless them, and then speak over them words about the vocational direction they were destined for. Then, it was the parents' responsibility to see that each child had the training and resources necessary to fulfill that purpose.

I've seen the campuses of many large ministries over the years. The sanctuary and multimedia centers are usually the crown jewels of the tour. But that's not so for affluent synagogues. If we were to tour those facilities, the leadership might show us their auditorium, but we would quickly see that their pride would be their library. Not only would we find a wide range of theological books there, but we would also discover college preparatory books for about every vocation imaginable. In addition, these vast libraries support parents in their God-given mission to train their children according to their strengths.

There is no mystery as to why many Jewish children tend to grow up to excel in academia, science, and business. For the most part, their parents have diligently prayed for them and trained them for success. There is no so-called Jewish conspiracy here as to why their children excel, just God's instruction and much work.

As mentioned earlier, part of the *Ev Shabbat* celebration on Friday evenings includes the father teaching his family the ways of God, the blessing over the children, and the parents speaking blessings over one another in front of the children. In that way, the father and mother become a united force in their children's eyes. This united front also plays out during the week as each parent supports the other.

From personal experience, I know I could not have accomplished what I have in life and ministry without my wonderful wife, Mary Lou. She is the other half of who I am (and the one with the most common sense). I cherish her wisdom and insights on interpersonal relationships and prophetic subjects. Even writing my books would not be possible without Mary. I struggle with dyslexia, which shows up more in my writing than in my reading. As a young child, I learned how things should read and rewrote them in my head as I was reading stories. This served me well until I started writing. Then, on paper or screen, I would see what I *meant* to say instead of what I had written. I've prayerfully been working on this issue. Mary served as my editor with *The Shinar Directive*, and my struggles with dyslexia brought her to tears many times. I faced the same challenges with our syndicated podcast, *The Kingdom*

Intelligence Briefing. I tried to handle it alone for about a year, but the podcast came to life when we started doing the show together. We share our hearts, laugh, pray, and cry together during the podcasts, and our listeners laugh, pray, and cry along with us. If I live to be one hundred, I will not have enough time to express how much I appreciate my wife. When a husband and wife accept their team roles, life becomes more precious and powerful.

I also complement Mary with my theological knowledge and academic background. I tend to be more theologically oriented, whereas Mary is more prophetic. We bring balance to one another. We don't make any major decisions unless we have discussed them, prayed about them, and come to a consensus. After forty years of marriage, I can testify that every time we've processed significant decisions together, not only have they turned out to be the right decisions, but the blessings of God have saturated those decisions as well.

So, husbands and wives serve as a "leadership team" over the gates of their home. Each partner sees issues from different perspectives. In other words, if a husband has a blind spot in a certain area, his wife can usually see more clearly in that area, and vice versa. There is no greater authority in the home than the husband and wife. No pastor, politician, or whatever title we can create has a higher authority than the husband-and-wife duo. It's time for this divinely inspired and sanctioned team to retake their spiritual and moral positions in the home. They alone are the final decision-makers regarding what's allowed and what's not allowed in their home: spiritually, emotionally, and physically.

Local Elders

The Holy Spirit has been emphasizing two ideas to me lately regarding the elders and the Church:

1. **Elders should be spiritually and theologically minded.** A lack of training for those called to serve in Gospel ministry is a personal soapbox

issue of mine. For decades, my family has lived in the Ozark Mountains, where there are numerous small, independent churches. In these tiny congregations, it is common to see folks commit their lives to Christ (be saved) one week, surrender serving in the ministry the next week, and ordained (officially invest with the authority to be a minister) the third week. This does not follow the biblical standard. The New Testament instructs us:

> This is a faithful saying: If a man desires the position of a bishop, he desires a good work. A bishop then must be blameless, the husband of one wife, temperate, sober-minded, of good behavior, hospitable, able to teach; not given to wine, not violent, not greedy for money, but gentle, not quarrelsome, not covetous; one who rules his own house well, having his children in submission with all reverence (for if a man does not know how to rule his own house, how will he take care of the church of God?); **not a novice**, lest being puffed up with pride he fall into the same condemnation as the devil. Moreover he must have a good testimony among those who are outside, lest he fall into reproach and the snare of the devil. (1 Timothy 3:1–7, emphasis added)

Remember, it was the Apostle Paul who said:

> Be diligent to present yourself approved to God, a worker who does not need to be ashamed, rightly dividing the word of truth. (2 Timothy 2:15)

Paul was a profound Bible scholar. In modern terms, we might consider him a minister with a double PhD from the "School of Hillel." At the feet of Gamaliel, he was thoroughly trained in the teachings of the First Testament and Greek philosophy (while being shown the superiority of God's instruction over the wisdom of humankind). This scholarship would be interwoven into the learning experience of any minister he personally mentored. For example, Timothy had not only known the Scriptures from his childhood, but was trained by a Jewish scholar. If ministers took their roles as a theologians and scholars more seriously, how many false doctrines would die before they even had a chance to be taught to churchgoers? Elders should guard their flocks—their students—against the winds of doctrine that the fallen immortals breathe through the cultures of society.

Decades ago, I listened to a teacher named Malcolm Smith. Several times, members of a congregation asked him to teach them how to properly interpret the Bible. He began his series of instruction with a warning, "If I properly train you to interpret the Bible, this congregation will be a challenge for every future pastor or visiting minister you will ever have again." He knew that when a congregation understands the science of hermeneutics (principles of biblical interpretation), they begin rejecting 90 percent of what is preached from pulpits. This lack of proper hermeneutics is especially true for many ministers who appear on national and international television, leading to the conclusion that much of evangelical Christianity has lost its way. Theologian Francis Schaeffer shared ten stumbling blocks for the evangelical Church in his book, *The Great Evangelical Disaster*. Here is a summary of his concerns provided by *Evangelical Focus Magazine*:

1. Growing Relativism
Relativism came about due to the Enlightenment's focus upon the autonomy of man. No longer was God to set the rules and call the shots; but rather humankind was to determine what was good and evil, true and false. Ethics and epistemology became absorbed by an inordinate passion for egoism and self-interest. Once the infallible, inerrant Word of God was openly decried; there was nothing left to take its place but human fancies.

Schaeffer realized that a church built upon the sandy-foundation of relativism could not withstand the onslaught of fallen reason. Only the non-negotiable absolutes of Scripture could enable the church to keep waging a good warfare. It was those "absolutes which enabled the early church to withstand the pressure of the Roman Empire." A relativistic church would have nothing left to say to a sinful culture.

2. Lack of Discipline

Given the resurgence of pagan relativism throughout post-modern society, many churches had fallen into the trap of downplaying Christian doctrine (absolutes) by refusing to take action against false teachers. Schaeffer identified a lack of church discipline as the real breeding ground for heretics. It was this deficiency which explained the victory of the liberal party within early twentieth-century American Presbyterianism.

As Schaeffer makes clear, "Discipline had not been consistently applied by the faithful men of the church." Without ecclesiastical and denominational discipline for doctrinal reasons, the church would be left vulnerable before the avalanche of false teaching.

Hence Schaeffer's proposal: "The practice of the purity of the visible church first means discipline of those who do not take a proper position in regard to the teaching of Scripture." And again: "Where there is a departure from the historic view of Scripture and from obedience to God's Word, then those who take this weakened view need to be brought under discipline." Only a high view of Scripture could justify the reestablishment of biblical discipline. If unorthodox ministers were not dealt with, how could their churches stay true to sound doctrine?

3. Compromise

Christians, according to Schaeffer, are supposed to take a stand for the truth. But the sad mark of his age was one of continual compromise on all fronts, both doctrinal and practical. Schaeffer was upset that many servants of the Lord were no longer willing to confront society with the truth of God. Such a spirit of indifference was leading the church down the slippery slope of apostasy.

Schaffer states:

> Truth carries with it confrontation. Truth demands confrontation; loving confrontation, but confrontation nevertheless. If our reflex action is always accommodation regardless of the centrality of the truth involved, there is something wrong.

Without a heartfelt faithfulness to the truth, claims of Scripture as witnessed in the lives of theological giants like B. B. Warfield (1851–1921), James Orr (1844–1913), and J. Gresham Machen (1881–1937), evangelicalism would not be able to prepare its children for the challenges accompanying the dark days ahead.

4. Social Work

Instead of keeping focused on the Gospel, many evangelical churches were running off in the liberal direction of "confusing the kingdom of God with a socialistic program." Without denying the importance of helping the downtrodden, Schaeffer was worried at how many ministers were basing their worldview on Marxist doctrine and not upon that of Scripture.

Sin, in Schaeffer's view, was not down to unjust social structures but to man's intrinsic wickedness. Iniquity abounded amongst both the poor and the wealthy. The idea of man's autonomous perfectibility did not stem from Scripture but from a fallen, man-centred Enlightenment philosophy. Even in countries where communist principles had ruled the political world, the results were disastrous with millions massacred on the altar of socialism. So Schaeffer quipped, "A socialistic program is not the answer." Of course churches need to help the poor; but she must keep first things first i.e. the proclamation of the forgiveness of sins through the Lord Jesus Christ.

5. The Temptation of Ecumenism

The World Council of Churches' (WCC) call to ecumenical unity greatly disturbed Schaeffer. As well as the pro-Marxist leanings of the WCC, the ecumenical movement was devoid of theological conviction. Every type of non-biblical theological fantasy was being permitted for the love of church unity i.e. Dorothee Sölle's (1929–2003) rejection of the Lord of Scripture; God being changed from a "Heavenly Father" into a "Celestial Mother"; and non-Christian religions being extolled as means of access to the divine, etc.

This was nothing other than false prophesy. The WCC was becoming a source of theological poison, promoting another Gospel which was no Gospel at all. Only a solid stance on an infallible and an inerrant Bible could bring down the flimsy walls of the WCC camp.

6. Abortion

Far from assenting to rife abortion-justifying euphemisms such as the "quality of life" or "the happiness and well-being of the mother" or "the need for every child to be wanted," Schaeffer believed that mass abortion was simply the outworking of a revived hedonistic attitude which put a person's happiness above a sacred respect for human life. He was unable to understand how anyone confessing the name of Christ could remain within a pro-abortion denomination.

In the final analysis, abortion was an all-out attack on the precious image of God which is made known through humankind. The unborn child is a human being created in the image of God, and to deny this is to deny the authority of the Bible. It is impossible to read Psalm 139 and truly believe what it says without realizing that life in the womb is human life. It is impossible to truly believe in the Incarnation and not realize that the child conceived in Mary by the power of the Holy Spirit was indeed the Son of God from the time of conception.

7. Liberalism

The fruit of theological liberalism had left many formerly-sound churches completely destitute of any spiritual power. Modernism, influenced by German Higher Criticism, had all but baptized the cardinal doctrines of the Enlightenment in the name of Christ. What did such an approach entail? Schaeffer answers: The denial of the supernatural; belief in the all-sufficiency of human reason; the rejection of the Fall; denial of the deity of Christ and his resurrection; belief in the perfectibility of man; and the destruction of the Bible.

Liberal preachers like the acclaimed Harry Emerson Fosdick (1878–1969) had no authoritative Bible left to preach from. Secular humanism took centre stage therefore any doctrine that did not put the spotlight upon man was ultimately done away with. Rather than the church influencing the world; the world took the reins of the church into her Gospel-denying grasp.

8. Hedonism

Hedonism is the philosophy that the meaning of life ultimately revolves around one's happiness, pleasure and feeling good at the moment. This hedonistic thrust had led contemporary society to cast off Christian morality in the name of self-fulfillment. Schaeffer was alarmed at how one's personal welfare was gradually taking primacy over human life i.e. as in the case of abortion. As Schaeffer spells out. We are surrounded by a society with no fixed standards and "no-fault" everything. Each thing is psychologically pushed away or explained away so that there is no right or wrong. And, as with the "happiness" of the mother taking precedence over human life, so anything which interferes with the "happiness" of the individual or society is dispensed with.

Hedonism's selfish and amoral nature was a real danger facing the church of Schaeffer's day and the same truth abides in our generation. In some places church has become more about 'customer satisfaction' than the true worship of the triune God.

9. The Loss of Propositional Revelation

Schaeffer insisted upon the need of a strong view of propositional revelation for the spiritual and academic welfare of contemporary Protestantism. Since God, the Creator of all things (language included), was truly there and had desired to communicate his Word to humankind, it was only natural that he should employ the medium of language and hence propositional sentences in order to make his will clear.

This meant that Schaeffer's stress was not primarily upon a believer's subjective religious experience, but upon the objective account of revelation displayed in Scripture. Experience was useful in the measure that it lined up with the teaching of the Bible. "What is our foundation?" asks Schaeffer. "It is that the infinite-personal God who exists has not been silent, but has spoken propositional truth in all that the Bible teaches." Take away propositional revelation and the foundation of the Christian is obliterated!

10. The Inerrant Scriptures

"We have an inerrant Scripture." A final key worry running throughout the whole of Schaeffer's volume is that of biblical inerrancy. He was incensed to hear of fellow evangelicals who were calling the plenary inspiration of Scripture into question by stressing that the Bible could contain geographical and historical errors despite its teaching upon religion and morals as being true (for the most part). This was the view of the Neo-Orthodox thinkers Karl Barth (1886–1968) and Emil Brunner (1889–1966).[84]

The elders in local congregations, Bible colleges, seminaries, and denominational leadership need to return to being scholars-in-residence for those under their charge. If we cast away sound biblical theology for the popular, how will we remain to be salt and light amid the cultures of Babylon?

2. **Elders and the church are the moral conscience of cities and nations.** Babylon cannot legislate morality. In today's world, the art of politics is primarily about who can lie the most convincingly to promote their hidden agenda. Politics is not the answer, but neither are the halls of higher education (unless they are thoroughly Christian and biblical). Historically, universities have been subject to "every wind of doctrine" promoted by the dark fallen spirits of the Second Heaven. Communists have used higher education to cripple and then topple nations from the start of their movement. Only the Church of the Living God can serve as the moral center or conscience of a city, state, or nation. Humanity is still eating from the tree of the knowledge of good and evil. Unrepentant men and women have rejected the leadership of the Creator and have demanded that they can decide for themselves what good or evil is. The mob rule of fallen humanity is where democracy fails. The crowd cannot rule because they can be manipulated into running off a cliff! A democratic republic is founded on righteous laws and then balanced with the voices of the people. Even the founding fathers were concerned about whether the colonies were moral enough to handle a democratic republic. Only after the great revivals of Jonathan Edwards and George Wakefield did the founders believe that they could move forward. The Constitution rested upon the moral foundation that the Church established through these Great Awakenings. Through the Gospel of the Kingdom, self-governance is only for the regenerated soul (and renewed mind).

A set of biblical moral standards is not a moving target. Moses would remind us that at least ten of these standards were written in stone by the finger of God. (The Ten Commandments also serve as a summation of all 613 commandments of the Torah.) Moral relativism is a lie of the dragon to move us away from the truth of God into Satan's unreality filled with misery, shame, and hopelessness. For the Church to become a light for those caught in darkness, we must stand immovable regarding God's truth. We must refuse to quarrel with lost people, but always speak God's truth in love.

> Flee also youthful lusts; but pursue righteousness, faith, love, peace with those who call on the Lord out of a pure heart. But avoid foolish and ignorant disputes, knowing that they generate strife. And a servant of the Lord must not quarrel but be gentle to all, able to teach, patient, in humility correcting those who are in opposition, if God perhaps will grant them repentance, so that they may know the truth, and that they may come to their senses and escape the snare of the devil, having been taken captive by him to do his will. (2 Timothy 2:22–26)

The local elders must proclaim God's truth, even in the face of an approaching storm of error. Years ago, I taught a class called "The Life of Faith" for the Biblical Life College and Seminary. The one truth the Holy Spirit impressed upon me to repeat to the point of becoming tedious was, "Whatever you compromise to gain, you will always lose." How much ground has the modern evangelical movement lost because it has continually compromised with the changing winds of Babylon? Every compromise has been reached because some have been convinced it would help them and the Church remain culturally relevant. This premise is a lie from the enemy. We stay relevant only by becoming the "other" culture or kingdom. Various shades of gray have no purpose in a world lost in darkness. Only the light of God's truth can stand in contrast to the chaos and confusion of the enemy. In the attempt to become more relevant, many of our churches have become irrelevant!

3. Elders as watchmen on the wall. I believe there are prophetic gifts within members of the Body of Christ. When I refer to the "prophetic," I'm not talking about to the writing of new Scripture. Quite the opposite: The Word of God is a complete revelation, from Genesis to Revelation, and needs no "new" additions. Nor am I referring to the "bless me" prophets who are proliferating today. Instead, I believe that true prophets in the Body of Christ serve as watchmen on the wall. David Wilkerson, author of *The Cross and the Switchblade* and *The Vision*, founder of Teen Challenge, and senior pastor of the Times Square Church, was such a prophet, but the Body of Christ largely rejected his message. In fact, Wilkerson was so rejected and scorned over the vision God gave him that he took his books regarding them out of print sometime in the late 1990s. Yet, with frightening regularity, the things he warned about are unfolding before our eyes today.

We see an example of a prophet serving as a watchman on the wall in the book of Acts:

> Then one of them, named Agabus, stood up and showed by the Spirit that there was going to be a great famine throughout all the world, which also happened in the days of Claudius Caesar. Then the disciples, each according to his ability, determined to send relief to the brethren dwelling in Judea. This they also did, and sent it to the elders by the hands of Barnabas and Saul. (Acts 11:28–30)

Because of a prophet named Agabus, an untold number of believers were saved from starvation.

Where were the prophets when we needed to be warned a new, satanically empowered communist wave called the "woke" movement would move through our society? How about the ongoing invasion and armed conflict that would arise at our nation's southern border? Concerning the first point, I have yet to run across a prophet who warned about "wokeness." I do know at least one prophetic voice that has warned of the coming armed conflict at the southern border. Unfortunately, his warning isn't popular in the Church, just as David Wilkerson's warnings weren't accepted. Too many of us prefer to line up to listen to those who follow the pattern of the Gnostics that have amazing stories of Jell-O mountains in Heaven, or about how rich God will make all of us. Because there is no fear of God in our gatherings, we've allowed our watchmen to be replaced with parrots that continually cry, "All is well."

Now let's deal with the other side of the prophetic spectrum. I am not a doom-and-gloom prophet. While I do believe that judgment is coming, provision is always made for the remnant. Too many prophets continually prophesy absolute destruction while providing no hope for God's people. When we examine the great biblical body of evidence on the operation of God's prophets (the First Testament), we discover the balance God instilled in His servants. Metaphorically speaking, it was as if the prophets had one foot in Heaven and the other on earth— among God's people. When the weight of the prophet was on the foot in Heaven, they would mourn and cry out for judgment because of how the people treated their covenant with God. When the prophet's weight shifted to the foot that was among God's people, he would cry out for mercy and repentance and do everything in his power to see that his prophetic words of judgment never came to pass. God's prophetic Word, through His prophets, outlined what would happen if they did not repent, called for the people to repent, and offered hope for the remnant if the judgment did indeed fall. The same is true with the book of Revelation. This prophetic book was for the bondservants of Jesus (Revelation 1:1). (As a side note, no reference in the book of Revelation indicates that it was written for those "left behind.") This powerful book by the Apostle John outlines the great cosmic conflict between the Creator and the Great Dragon (Satan). This book contains correction, calls for repentance, assurance that God will win, and comfort that, one day, God will wipe every tear from our eyes and place us in a New Heaven and New Earth that this conflict has never touched. Revelation is a book of hope for God's people in every generation. As the days approach its ultimate unfolding upon the stage of history, its message of hope is needed for God's people today.

A Call to Biblical Balance

From elders at home, elders in the cities, and prophets on the walls, there is a biblical balance. But, unfortunately, when our traditions or the fickle currents of culture controlled by Hell move us away from God's instruction, we open ourselves to the enemy's attacks. The only way to reverse this trend is to return to biblical standards, drive out the tacit influence of the enemy, and begin conducting our lives and ministries according to Kingdom principles. Then, and only then, can our perimeters be cleared of the enemy's covert operatives and our walls of protection rebuilt and fortified.

Maintaining the proper lines of authority in the home and assembly and defending against false teachings are all essential elements of spiritual warfare.

Prayer

Father, it is time to rebuild the walls of protection and reestablish the gates in my home, ministry, and community. Please forgive me for relinquishing my positions as elder and watchman. Give me the grace to take up the mantles of authority you have given to me, and teach me to move in Kingdom authority, in Jesus' name.

Review Questions

1. In the ancient world, why were the walls and gates so important to the cities?
2. What did the gates of the cities include?
3. In Matthew 18:15–20, what type of binding and loosing was Jesus referring to?
4. How are the elders to serve in our local assemblies?
5. How are parents to serve as elders in their homes?
6. What is a balanced approach to the male's leadership in marriage?
7. What two positions can cause a husband's leadership to get out of biblical balance?
8. How does leadership in the home function best?
9. What three areas do local and national elders need to focus on?
10. What is the danger of moral relativism?
11. How are modern-day prophets and watchmen to function?

THE SPIRITUAL REALITY
OF SOUL TIES

*Therefore a man shall leave his father and mother and
be joined to his wife, and they shall become one flesh.*

GENESIS 2:24

Since the beginning, there has been a divine mystery regarding the union of a man and woman under the marriage covenant. This mystery was so powerful that the Apostle Paul used it as an example of the relationship between Christ and the Church.

Therefore, just as the church is subject to Christ, so let the wives be to their own husbands in everything. Husbands, love your wives, just as Christ also loved the church and gave Himself for her, that He might sanctify and cleanse her with the washing of water by the word, that He might present her to Himself a glorious church, not having spot or wrinkle or any such thing, but that she should be holy and without blemish. So husbands ought to love their own wives as their own bodies; he who loves his wife loves himself. For no one ever hated his own flesh, but nourishes and cherishes it, just as the Lord does the church. For

189

we are members of His body, of His flesh and of His bones. **For this reason a man shall leave his father and mother and be joined to his wife, and the two shall become one flesh.** This is a great mystery, but I speak concerning Christ and the church. (Ephesians 5:24–32, emphasis added)

Physical intimacy, a natural part of the marriage covenant, is beautiful. Sexual intimacy within the boundaries of the marriage covenant was God's idea and ideal from the very beginning.

Sexual union is a powerful act. I believe this is one of the reasons the mystery religions so abuse it. The very act engages a spiritual power that should only be released within the biblical confines of the marriage covenant.

The ancient sages of Israel have pondered the words used by Adam in Genesis 2:24. What captured their attention, in particular, was a specific Hebrew word used by Adam: one or *'echad* (ekh-awd'). This Hebrew word is used in a significant passage of Scripture dealing with the concept of the Godhead:

Hear, O Israel: The LORD our God, the LORD is one! (Deuteronomy 6:4)

This isn't just any ordinary verse for the Jewish people; it is a verse of supreme importance. This passage is the beginning of the Shema Prayer and serves historically as the watchword for the nation of Israel. We have not entirely understood the spiritual dynamic in the marriage relationship.

Humanity was created as a triune being. We are a spirit, we have a soul, and we live in a body. Sexual union is more than just two bodies connecting. There is an intertwining of the couple's spirits, souls, and bodies. As a couple builds a life together, their intimacy forges a new oneness. Two lives become one life—lived together. Their strengths support one another, and they provide a cover or shield for one another's weaknesses. From the story of Genesis, we discover that two become one and, in so doing, each becomes complete, or whole.

There is what has been called a "soul tie" established in the marriage. The spiritual or emotional strength of one can flow to the other. Intimacy creates a spiritual bridge between the two with a divine purpose. God meant this original dynamic of the marriage soul ties to be wonderful and empowering. However, sin entered the Garden, and it changed everything.

> Or do you not know that he who is joined to a harlot is one body with her? For "the two," He says, "shall become one flesh." (1 Corinthians 6:16, emphasis added)

In 1 Corinthians 6:16, Paul addresses former pagans who had become Christians. His words must have had a certain level of "shock and awe" for them. While the Hebrews interwove God's instruction into the very culture so that the standard was no sexual relations until marriage and no sexual relations outside of marriage; the pagan world adhered to precisely the opposite! Fornication was part of their religious practices. Nothing was off-limits in the pagan world: young children, slaves, family members (to include your own children), and even animals. According to Roman law, the only restrictions involved social status and who could do what to whom. Believe it or not, this is precisely where the current satanic rave is attempting to take us. In both the US and European countries, there are those seeking to make all sexual practices mainstream and protected by law. These agents of darkness are attempting to reverse the effects of the Judeo-Christian ethic and return us to the pagan worldview of sexuality from Babylon!

What the Apostle Paul revealed in 1 Corinthians 6:16 should be terrifying to any discerning believer. If we were sexually active before marriage (or if we commit adultery after marriage), we don't just have a soul tie with our spouse; we are plugged into a network of soul ties. Imagine for a moment what Paul is revealing here. If we sleep with a harlot, we become connected to everyone she has ever slept with—and then everyone that person has slept with. Instead of a single soul tie with the love of our life, we are plugged into a spiritual network that would cause the network specialist company Cisco Technologies to become green with envy! Unfortunately, too many believers are walking around with spiritual sexually transmitted diseases and wonder why they cannot make significant progress in their spiritual growth. For those struggling, if they could research their sexual multi-level network, it is possible that they would discover someone in the occult.

Michael J. Norton shares this possible network of souls in his book, *Field Guide to Spiritual Warfare: Pull the Impossible*:

> We live in a promiscuous society. The number of soul ties from casual encounters with opposite-sex partners is staggering. Add to that the number of soul ties that slip in through homosexual relationships.
>
> Studies have shown that the average heterosexual male in a steady, married, but promiscuous relationship, in the Netherlands, can have as many as eight relationships per year. A homosexual male can have as many as several hundred.[1] No matter how you look at the numbers, they get really big really fast—especially because you can take on soul ties with people you have never even met.
>
> Here's how this works: Imagine that you are a single woman who has had one sexual encounter this year. Let's assume that your one-night stand was with a promiscuous man who had intercourse with eight other women over the course of the year. For the sake of argument, imagine that each of these women had sex with as many as eight men that year.
>
> Your one-night stand did not expose you to one soul tie with your only partner. When you had sex with him, you were exposed to all of the soul ties from all of his sexual encounters. In this case, you can take on as many as 64 soul ties, mostly with

people you will never meet—and we are singling out just one year's worth of promiscuous sexual activity!

Keep in mind that some homosexuals engage in casual opposite-sex relationships from time to time. Now consider what happens if your one-night stand involves a man who has slept with another woman who, in turn, had relations with a homosexual man. There's no telling what kind of exponential exposure to soul ties you would be risking. Notice that we have not even taken into account the possibilities of exposure to sexually transmitted diseases.[85]

The Case of a Suicidal Church Elder

Years ago, I oversaw the Marriage and Family Therapy graduate programs at Biblical Life College and Seminary. One of my students was a pastor of a mainstream evangelical church. He called me desperately seeking answers that would help one of his elders. This man had been a pillar in the church and the community for years. Now, the elder was fighting the urge to attempt suicide. The man admitted to the pastor that he was fighting homosexual urges that seemed to be coming out of nowhere, pushing him toward suicide. After some tense sessions with the pastor, the man confessed to having an affair with a woman half his age in the congregation. The pastor and his wife then confronted the woman. She finally admitted she was a practicing Wiccan who had been sent to the church to derail the congregation's effectiveness in the community. How can an affair with the opposite sex result in same-sex desires? The practices of Wicca include bisexual relationships (although not all Wiccans would necessarily do so). This man had created a soul tie with a young woman who had sexual relationships with both men and women. Her desires manifested in his life as an almost overwhelming desire for a homosexual relationship. Once the elder repented and broke the soul tie, the desires left him. It was another five years before the student graduated from the program and moved on academically. In those five years, this elder never experienced those desires again (and he became one of the most faithful men imaginable).

Besides being sexually active before marriage or having an affair after entering marriage, we need to deal with those who have suffered the tragedy of divorce. Unless, as a part of post-divorce or premarital counseling, the divorcee has been led in a prayer to break the soul tie with his or her former mate, the connection remains. This connection to a former mate can significantly hamper building a new life.

Several waves of demonic influence slowly took hold of America after World War II. First, there were the Kinsey studies in 1948 and 1953. In his documentary, *The Kinsey Syndrome: How One Man Destroyed the Morality of America,* Chris Pinto points out that Kinsey's research was severely flawed. Much of his research was gathered from pedophiles and prostitutes and had no connection to the general population. Nevertheless, the Kinsey Institute had a leading role in how our courts and schools of higher learning began to view sexuality (to include what was considered at the time as deviant sexual behavior). Kinsey's reports paved the way for the sexual revolution of the 1960s and the one we are experiencing today. Since the initial release of the Kinsey report, America has been on a slow moral decline. If we could see the soul-tie network individuals have been building in this new sexual culture, it would be alarming.

It is time to repent, remove ungodly sexual soul ties, and restore the standard the Creator established in His Word. Hebrews 13:4 tell us:

Marriage is honorable among all, and the bed undefiled; but fornicators and adulterers God will judge.

The Greek word used for "undefiled" is *amiantos* [*am-ee'-an-tos*], which means "not defiled, unsoiled; free from that by which the nature of a thing is deformed and debased, or its force and vigor impaired." [86] The website Got Questions: Your Questions—Biblical Answers features an insightful article on Hebrews 13:4:

Chapter 13 is the concluding chapter of the book of Hebrews and ends with a series of final exhortations to Christians. Verse 4 says, "Marriage is to be held in honor among all, and the marriage bed is to be undefiled; for fornicators and adulterers God will judge" (NASB). The Greek word translated "undefiled" is only used in this exact form four times in the New Testament, and it means "uncontaminated" or "set apart." Hebrews 7:26 uses this word to describe Jesus Christ, our high priest, and James 1:27 says that "undefiled" religion is that which helps widows and orphans and remains unstained by the world.

The marriage bed is to be kept pure or undefiled. In other words, the sexual intimacy shared between a husband and wife is to be reserved for that couple alone. God created the sexual union to be between a husband and a wife. Period. Only. No other use of sexuality is ever condoned in Scripture. To abuse or misuse God's gift of sex is to defile the marriage bed.

A marriage bed can be defiled in several ways:

1. **Fornication.** When two unmarried people engage in sexual intercourse, they are defiling God's good gift of sex. Those who have not vowed themselves to each other in a binding lifetime union have no right to exploit the culmination of such a vow. Sex was designed to be the final act of consecration when a couple pledge their lives to each other in a sacred covenant. All forms of sexuality outside a marriage union are bringing dishonor to the honorable institution of marriage (1 Corinthians 6:18).

2. **Adultery.** When one or both parties in a sexual union are married to someone else, God calls their sexual acts adultery. Adultery was punishable by death under God's Old Covenant with Israel (Deuteronomy 22:22; Leviticus 20:10). Even though we no longer live under that covenant, adultery is still high on

God's list of moral evils (Matthew 5:28, 32) and is always named as a sin that keeps unrepentant offenders from inheriting the kingdom of God (Galatians 5:19; 1 Corinthians 6:9).

3. **Homosexuality.** Another defilement of the marriage bed is the perversion of men having sex with men or women with women. Despite our world's current embrace of homosexual practice, this vile act has never been and will never be sanctioned or blessed by God. Homosexuality is a distortion of God's gift of physical unity between husband and wife and is the only sexual activity labeled an abomination (Leviticus 20:13). The prohibition against homosexuality carries right into the New Covenant, as it is listed with those sins that keep the unrepentant out of the kingdom of God (1 Corinthians 6:9; 1 Timothy 1:9–10; Jude 1:7).

4. **Prostitution.** Proverbs 7 gives a detailed look at the destruction that comes upon a young man who allows himself to be seduced by a harlot. The sin of harlotry is often used as a metaphor for unfaithful Israel (Hosea 4:15; Jeremiah 3:8; Judges 8:33). Christians are warned to avoid such immorality because of the sacredness of the marriage bed (1 Corinthians 6:15–16; Ephesians 5:3).

5. **Pornography.** Using pornography for sexual gratification is a more modern way to defile the marriage bed. Pornographic books, videos, sexting, and the use of other sexually explicit materials also defile the sanctity of the sexual union between a man and wife. Porn has the effect of bringing strangers into the bedroom, even if only through the eyes. Jesus warned that lust associated with *looking* at a woman is equivalent to adultery before God (Matthew 5:28). Pornography has elevated sexual

lust to an art form, but it is still corrupting to the heart and a sinful defiling of the sexual act.

God created human beings to be pure in body and spirit. Sexual union between a husband and wife was a part of that purity (Genesis 2:24–25). When Adam and Eve sinned, sexuality was tainted along with everything else. Jesus purchased the power to reclaim that purity through His sacrificial death on the cross (2 Corinthians 5:21). No sin, including sexual immorality, is too great for the power of that atoning death and resurrection to pardon. Even though we may have defiled the marriage bed in many ways, God can restore sexual purity and holiness when we repent and commit our lives to following Him (Psalm 51:7; 1 John 1:7).[87]

Have the currents of the sexual revolution polluted your marriage bed? If they have, the blood of Jesus is greater. We must repent and return to God's original instructions regarding our sexuality. It will deepen our relationship with our mates and free us from Babylon's tentacles!

Sexual relationships are not the only way soul ties can be established. Whom we form relationships with has a powerful effect on our lives.

Soul Ties and Nonsexual Relationships

A secondary type of soul tie is not sexual in nature. It is formed through the relationships around us outside of marriage. These secondary soul ties don't have the networking nature of sexual soul ties. (Although it should be noted that if a secondary soul tie is accompanied by a toxic mind virus [every wind of doctrine] empowered by the kingdom of darkness, it can establish a hive mind or groupthink.] It has been noted that, during the French revolution, the nation became insane and bloodthirsty. The spirit behind this French Revolution's mind virus fed off

hatred and carnage. Since we have already dealt with mind viruses, I
want to concentrate on interpersonal relationships.

John Eckhardt defines "soul ties" in his book, *Deliverance and Spiritual Warfare Manual*, as:

A bond between two individuals. The souls (mind, will, emotions) of individuals knit or joined together. A bond, a joining
together of souls for good or evil. There are godly and ungodly
soul ties.[88]

Eckhardt continues his discussion regarding soul ties:

Soul ties are formed as a result of relationships with people. There
are godly and ungodly soul ties. Ungodly soul ties cause a person
to be manipulated and controlled by another person, causing
the person to live in disobedience to God. There are godly soul
ties as well: "The soul of Jonathan was knit with the soul of
David, and Jonathan loved him as his own life" (1 Samual 18:1,
AMP). Ungodly soul ties are Satan's counterfeits of good relationships and unions with godly people. (See 1 Corinthians 6:16;
2 Corinthians 6:14)

Soul ties cause:
- One person to follow another (Ruth 1:14–16)
- A person to fulfill the desires of another (1 Sam. 20:4)
- A person to surrender his goods to another (1 Sam.
  18:4)
- A person to react in anger when the person to whom
  they are soul tied to is attacked (1 Sam. 20:34)
- A person to protect another in times of danger (1 Sam.
  20:35–40)
- Loyalty between a leader and his followers (2 Sam. 20:2).

Ungodly soul ties can:

- Be formed through fornication (Gen. 34:1–3)
- Cause you to have a check in your spirit (2 Chron. 18:1–6)
- Cause your works to be destroyed (2 Chron. 20:35–37)
- Be formed through witchcraft (Gal. 3:1; 4:17)
- Turn a person's heart away from God (1 Kings 11:1–4)

Good soul ties can be destroyed through witchcraft (Gal. 4:15–16). There is also a demonic spirit that destroys good soul ties called the "Good Soul-Tie Breaker." There are also spirits of false love that cause people who are not in love to marry, thus forming a bad soul tie.

Ungodly soul ties are relationships that are based on lust, witchcraft, domination, and bondage. Godly soul ties are relationships that edify and are based on love (Col. 2:2).

Demon spirits can be transferred from one person to another through the avenue of soul ties. Spirits of the Lord can also be transferred this way.

Godly soul ties are created by the Lord between a pastor and his members to help him carry out the vision or plan that God has placed in his heart. This soul tie becomes a channel through which the pastor can feed them with knowledge and understanding (Jer. 3:15). Spirits of wisdom, knowledge, and understanding are transferred through this godly soul tie. God joins people to certain ministries that will cause them to willingly submit to His authority and help carry out His vision.[89]

The Apostle Paul warned the believers in Corinth:

Do not be deceived: "Evil company corrupts good habits." Awake to righteousness, and do not sin; for some do not have the knowledge of God. I speak this to your shame. (1 Corinthians 15:33–34)

Adam Clarke shares how this same warning of the Apostle Paul transcends cultures:

> **Evil communications corrupt good manners**—There are many sayings like this among the Greek poets; but this of the apostle, and which according to the best MSS. makes an Iambic verse, is generally supposed to have been taken from Menander's lost comedy of Thais.
>
> Φθείρουσιν ηθη χρησθ᾽ ὁμιλιαι κακαι·
>
> Bad company good morals doth corrupt.
>
> There is a proverb much like this among the rabbis:
>
> אכיטרל ישיכי ורקוא אכיטר רתו ישיכי ירוא ירח
>
> "There were two dry logs of wood, and one green log; but the dry logs burnt up the green log."[90]

We need to be careful of the relationships we forge. The deeper the relationship, the more substantial the established soul ties. When we establish relationships with individuals who have a deep walk with God, the dynamic of that relationship will draw us into new depths with the Almighty.

> As iron sharpens iron, so a man sharpens the countenance of his friend. (Proverbs 27:17)

The reverse is also true. Toxic individuals create toxic soul ties. How many times have we seen good people who have been drawn into self-destructive behavior because they fell into the wrong crowd? There are many reasons that someone, unfortunately, creates a soul tie with someone who isn't walking with God or claims to be but has destructive strongholds. The stronghold of the toxic individual can touch something in an individual's carnal nature. Like cultural strongholds, a mind virus can easily ride on the carriers of the lust of the flesh, the lust of the eyes, and the pride of life.

We could use many examples on both a personal and group basis. How many congregations have had prayer meetings that started in the fire of God but, over time, descended into nothing more than sessions of gossip and complaining? Somewhere in the life cycle of that group, an individual entered its orbit with a stronghold that eventually established sufficient soul ties with members until the group became toxic. Kingdom warriors must always be watchful against such inroads by the enemy. Remember, the kingdom of darkness loves to use strongholds in believers to turn them into covert operators, whether or not they're aware of it.

Jesus' Pattern of Relationships

Over the years, I've studied the science of leadership and, when approaching the subject from a biblical perspective, I've noted that Jesus had circles of influence. In some circles, He was more open than in others.

Public Circles:

- General Population
- Religious Leaders

Personal Circles:

- The seventy: Jesus sends out seventy disciples to minister.
- The twelve: The twelve apostles.
- The three: Transfiguration—John, Peter, and James.
- The one: John—the one Jesus trusted with His mother's care.
- The Ultimate One: God.

What has been amazing to me is that in all of these relationships (except for God), Jesus was immovable. He was always the One who was affecting others, whether calling them on the carpet, calling them to repent and walk in the Kingdom, or calling them to a deeper understanding of the

Word. Jesus never allowed interpersonal relationships to alter who He was and His actions. There was no drunken revelry, even when the religious leaders accused Him of eating with sinners. Instead, these "sinners" were captivated by their discussion with Jesus.

I believe Jesus maintained this balance (as our example) because He was firmly established in the most significant soul tie that could ever possibly exist: His relationship with the Father. In every relationship Jesus had, His Father was right there with Him.

There is a beautiful tradition among the Jewish people as they begin to close out the Sabbath: they light the *Havdalah* candle. This braided candle represents the intertwining of the hearts of God's people with each other and with God that occurs on the Sabbath. What a powerful example for the believer. If our hearts are adequately intertwined with God's, it inoculates us from ungodly soul ties and the mind viruses of the enemy.

At the end of this chapter, I will provide a prayer to break ungodly soul ties. But make no mistake: this is just half of the equation. The other half of the solution is that God must be in every relationship. Not only is God the primary soul tie, but He and His Kingdom also become filters for our soul and our relationships.

Havdalah candle

Though one may be overpowered by another, two can withstand him. And a threefold cord is not quickly broken. (Ecclesiastes 4:12)

For a marriage to be strong and maintain balance, God must be the one who holds everything together. In every relationship, the Apostle Paul warns:

Do not be unequally yoked together with unbelievers. For what fellowship has righteousness with lawlessness? And what communion has light with darkness? And what accord has Christ with Belial? Or what part has a believer with an unbeliever? And what agreement has the temple of God with idols? For you are the temple of the living God. As God has said: "**I will dwell in them and walk among them. I will be their God, and they shall be My people.**" (2 Corinthians 6:14–16, emphasis added)

While this Scripture in 2 Corinthians 6:14–16 is often used regarding marriage, in its biblical context, it refers to *all* relationships. The New American Standard Version translates verse 14 this way:

Do not be bound together with unbelievers; for what partnership have righteousness and lawlessness, or what fellowship has light with darkness?[91]

There is a difference between acquaintances and those we become bound to in the bonds of friendship. There must be circles of influence established in our lives. Acquaintances are in the far outer circle. I remember sitting at a *yeshiva* (a Jewish form of group study) hosted by Restoration Fellowship International Ministerial Association years ago. The discussion turned to the tent of Abraham and the tabernacle of Moses. Each structure has three elements: the outer court, an inner room for fellowship, and the most inner room.

Tent of Abraham	Tabernacle of Moses
Outer area to greet acquaintances.	Outer court for the general population.
Inner room for dining with friends.	Holy Place is set up like a dining room.
Bedroom and the marriage bed.	Holy of Holies where God's throne is and His glory dwell.

In ancient times, the tent of Abraham was modeled after the concept of levels of influences or circles of friends. Travelers and acquaintances would be greeted and entertained outside of the ten. Trusted friends and those with whom one had entered a salt covenant (covenant of deep friendship) were welcomed into the inner room to dine at the family table. We still see this tradition and expectation today in my Boomer generation (but not so much in the X, Y, and Z generation). If you are ever welcomed into a home and dine with the family, then turn against that family or speak evil of it, you are considered the lowest of the low. There is an Ozark expression for that. Since I don't want to give my editors at Defender Publishing an editorial crisis, we'll stick with something like "lower than a snake's belly." Finally, the marriage bed chamber is reserved for the one the marriage covenant is entered with. The bed chamber is a holy place that should never be violated.

How can we establish guidelines for who can be drawn into the inner circles? The preeminent principle must be God and His Kingdom. Even in marriage, it must be more than physical attraction or emotional compatibility; it must be because God is drawing the two together. We need to become Kingdom aware and be able to sense those who have developed the same level of intimacy with God. With that said, perhaps this is where the problem lies in the Church today. We develop shallow relationships with God and then try to fill the emptiness with more profound relationships with those around us. This spiritual imbalance in our relationships has slowly drawn us to where we are today: a toxic church that has departed from biblicity. The Protestant/evangelical movement we are privileged to be a part of was forged by a people whose primary mission was to know God and His Word. It was such a vital part of their lives that they were willing to die for their beliefs. Their movement was not church-centric or social-centric; it was utterly God-centric. If we are going to regain balance and become a hard target able to withstand the enemy's seduction, coercion, or blackmail, we need to return to the principle of abiding in Christ. Jesus is the Divine Vine, and we are the branches. We are supposed to be feeding off what the Vine provides, not on what we can draw from one another! Fellowship with other believers is good, but it is not the primary focus of the Kingdom warrior. The Kingdom warrior lives for God and would be willing to lay down his or her life for the sake of the Kingdom and its Gospel. This unique place is where the Kingdom, the anointing, and miracles can flow unhindered.

> On the last day, that great day of the feast, Jesus stood and cried out, saying, "If anyone thirsts, let him come to Me and drink. He who believes in Me, as the Scripture has said, out of his heart will flow rivers of living water." But this He spoke concerning the Spirit, whom those believing in Him would receive; for the Holy Spirit was not yet given, because Jesus was not yet glorified. (John 7:37–39)

The background behind John 7:37–39 is a powerful one. Adam Clarke provides insights into that day.

> **In the last day, that great day of the feast**—This was the eighth day, and was called the great day, because of certain traditional observances, and not on account of any excellence which it derived from the original institution. On the seven days they professed to offer sacrifices for the seventy nations of the earth, but on the eighth day they offered sacrifices for Israel; therefore the eighth day was more highly esteemed than any of the others. It is probably to this that the evangelist refers when he calls the last day the great day of the feast. It was probably when they went to draw water from the pool Siloam, and while they were pouring it out at the foot of the altar, that our Lord spoke these words; for, as that ceremony pointed out the gracious influences of the Holy Spirit, our Lord, who was the fountain whence it was to proceed, called the people to himself, that, by believing on him, they might be made partakers of that inestimable benefit.[92]

The road from the pool of Siloam was lined with people all the way to the Temple Mount with palm branches crying out "Hosanna." As the water vessels arrived before the blazing-hot, brazen altar, a holy hush came over the crowd. The hissing of the water could be heard hitting the burning altar. It was at that moment that Jesus cried out! It was a moment of the fire of God and the outpouring of the Spirit as water. Cold altars will not produce what Jesus was talking about! If the water is to flow correctly, it must flow from an altar that has the fire of God burning brightly. The River of Life can only flow from a heart that has fallen madly in love with Jesus, and this relationship alone is the primary one established in the believer's life.

We must examine all our relationships. Here are some questions that we need to ask ourselves:

✢ Is Christ our central core relationship, and is every other relationship aligned with Him?

✢ If not, we need to prioritize our circles of relationships. Some need to be moved to the outer rings, and others cut off entirely, if we are to move forward in the Kingdom.

✢ Have we appropriately invested in our relationship with our spouse, and is God genuinely established as the third cord in this intertwining of hearts?

Only the Holy Spirit and believers know the answers to these questions. As the distinctive warfare of the end times increases with each passing day, we must be honest with ourselves, clean house, and labor to build proper biblical relationships and establish our perimeter with Kingdom standards. The Kingdom alone will withstand the storm that is approaching.

Prayer 1: Breaking Physical Soul Ties

Father, my relationship with you must be my top priority in life. I ask you to forgive me for the times I have placed my relationships with others above our relationship. Help me draw closer to you and balance the Kingdom in my other relationships.

I believe the blood of Jesus cleanses me of all my sins. Therefore, I bring before you the soul ties I have made through physical union with the following people:
Name the individuals if you can:

_____

_____

I ask you to forgive me and release me from the consequences of these soul ties. I ask you to close the doorways opened by these soul ties and seal them with the blood of Jesus.

Now, in Jesus' name, I command any demons that have influenced my life through the doorways of soul ties to leave me now and forever. Satan, you can never use these doorways again. I remind you of the promise of the Word that says, "Whom the Son sets free is free indeed."

Father, I receive my release by faith and thank you for it, in Jesus' name.

Prayer 2: Realigning Relationships

Father, I ask you to forgive me for placing any relationship above my relationship with you. Draw me closer to you and give me the wisdom of your Spirit to realign my relationships with those around me with Kingdom principles. I ask that the blood of Jesus and the Kingdom serve as filters to any other relationship I have. May your Kingdom flow through me and affect those around me by causing them to become hungry for your presence.

I break any influence of the enemy established in my life through relationships with others who have strongholds of the enemy in their lives. I pull down every vain imagination that is against Christ or His Word.

Father, help me tear down any strongholds the enemy has established within me through wrong relationships and replace them with your Word and Your Spirit. I plead the blood of Jesus into those places within my soul and command them to line up with God's Word. I commit before you to meditate on your Word and fill those places in my soul with you and your Kingdom, in Jesus' name.

Prayer 3: To Strengthen the Relationship with the Spouse

Father, help me to rebuild a proper relationship with _____. This relationship is not to be before my relationship with you, but it is to be before any other relationship with anyone else. Please draw us closer to you, and then draw us closer to one another. I recommit to the marriage covenant that I have with _____, and I will open my heart and life to the spouse you have given me like never before. I ask that your Spirit would help me in this holy union. Heal my heart of anything that would separate me from _____, and help us to have a deeper and more meaningful relationship than ever before, in Jesus' name.

Review Questions

1. Is sexual union in marriage more than just a physical connection? If so, how?
2. How does the soul tie work in marriage?
3. What happens when we have sex outside of marriage?
4. What can defile the marriage bed?
5. What are nonsexual soul ties, and how can they affect us?
6. Are there both good and bad nonsexual soul ties?
7. What is the ultimate soul tie each believer must have?
8. What does the *Havdalah* candle represent?
9. How does our relationship with God bring balance to all of the other relationships in our lives?
10. What element is necessary for the living water of the Holy Spirit to flow correctly from the believer's life?

THE FEAR OF THE LORD

Covering Unknown Doors,
and Continued Vigilance

The fear of the LORD is the beginning of wisdom;
A good understanding have all those who do His
commandments. His praise endures forever.

PSALM 111:10

The fear of the LORD seems to be a lost concept for the modern
Church. Unfortunately, in our human-centric theology, we have
made for ourselves a version of God that is appealing to the flesh. Many
of our worship songs are about how God loves us just as we are (with
the false concept that there is no real need for change). The preaching of
the Gospel of the Kingdom has been replaced with a self-help gospel in
which Jesus is our coach and passes out warm fuzzies at the door as we
enter our houses of worship. Sin is no longer considered a sin, and we
have become jaundiced regarding the need for personal holiness to walk
with God.

The earth is the LORD'S, and all its fullness, the world and those
who dwell therein. For He has founded it upon the seas, and

established it upon the waters. Who may ascend into the hill
of the LORD? Or who may stand in His holy place? He who has
clean hands and a pure heart, who has not lifted up his soul to
an idol, nor sworn deceitfully. He shall receive blessing from the
LORD, and righteousness from the God of his salvation. This is
Jacob, the generation of those who seek Him, who seek Your
face. Selah. (Psalm 24:1–6)

We are no longer in reverent awe of a Creator so overwhelmingly
powerful and grand that even the universe cannot contain him. Solomon was the king of Israel, whom God had filled with supernatural wisdom. During the dedication of the Temple, Solomon had one singular
moment of perfect clarity when he declared:

But will God indeed dwell on the earth? Behold, heaven and
the heaven of heavens cannot contain You. How much less this
temple which I have built! (1 Kings 8:27)

At that moment, Solomon's eyes were opened and he realized that
the universe was not large enough to contain Almighty God. The Father
dwells in eternity. Theologically, eternity is a place outside of creation. It
is the secret place of Almighty God, and it is from there that He makes
Himself known to His creation. God's power is beyond our comprehen-
sion, and His presence has more splendor than we could ever imagine.
Even the angels who have beheld His face since the beginning of time
are suspended in a perpetual state of being overwhelmed by His majesty.

In the year that King Uzziah died, I saw the Lord sitting on a
throne, high and lifted up, and the train of His robe filled the
temple. Above it stood seraphim; each one had six wings: with
two he covered his face, with two he covered his feet, and with
two he flew. And one cried to another and said: "Holy, holy,

holy is the LORD of hosts; The whole earth is full of His glory!"
And the posts of the door were shaken by the voice of him who
cried out, and the house was filled with smoke. (Isaiah 6:1–4)

Then, in Revelation 4:6–11, the twenty-four elders are caught in the
same vortex of holy splendor:

Before the throne there was a sea of glass, like crystal. And in
the midst of the throne, and around the throne, were four living creatures full of eyes in front and in back. The first living
creature was like a lion, the second living creature like a calf, the
third living creature had a face like a man, and the fourth living
creature was like a flying eagle. The four living creatures, each
having six wings, were full of eyes around and within. And they
do not rest day or night, saying: "Holy, holy, holy, Lord God
Almighty, Who was and is and is to come!" Whenever the living
creatures give glory and honor and thanks to Him who sits on
the throne, who lives forever and ever, the twenty-four elders fall
down before Him who sits on the throne and worship Him who
lives forever and ever, and cast their crowns before the throne,
saying: "You are worthy, O Lord, To receive glory and honor
and power; For You created all things, And by Your will they
exist and were created." (Revelation 4:6–11)

And yet, on earth, we have become flippant with our relationship
with the Most High God. Over the past century, the priesthood of darkness has slowly and methodically injected humanistic and New-Age ide-
ologies to dilute the Gospel of the Kingdom and seduce many sections of
Christianity into developing idols that would appease their carnal nature.
Slowly, other gospels and versions of Jesus were developed for those that
had itching ears. Today, we have an epidemic of unsaved Christians who
have aligned themselves with the enemies of God. I remember watching

a news broadcast about abortion and Christianity. In the interview, the
reporter talked to a minister who represented the dark priesthood more
than the historic Church of the Living God. She made one statement in
the interview that encapsulated the belief system of the nearly apostate
church. She declared, "I would never serve a god that did not believe
that abortion was a sacred right or would inflict judgment on those that
do." Like Israel of old, what started out with an outpouring of the fire of
God has now embraced strange fire and has erected altars to Molech and
Ashtoreth. At that moment, I realized that the book of Revelation was
the fifth Gospel. This prophetic book is the revelation of Jesus Christ.
The apostate church is about to be reintroduced to a Holy God they
once served, and it will not be pretty.

The one who penned the book of Revelation was the Apostle John.
In Jesus' circles of influence, John was at the human center. It was young
John who laid his head on the chest of Jesus during the Last Supper and
heard the heartbeat of God. Jesus, as Mary's firstborn son, was responsible for caring for His mother. While giving His life for humanity on
the cross, it was John whom He entrusted with Mary's care. So, if any
human being was close to Jesus, it was John. John had seen and walked
with the Risen Messiah before the Ascension, and he had seen Jesus
enter into the clouds. Now, consider John's response when he sees his
Risen Lord again:

> Then I turned to see the voice that spoke with me. And having
> turned I saw seven golden lampstands, and in the midst of the
> seven lampstands One like the Son of Man, clothed with a gar-
> ment down to the feet and girded about the chest with a golden
> band. His head and hair were white like wool, as white as snow,
> and His eyes like a flame of fire; His feet were like fine brass, as if
> refined in a furnace, and His voice as the sound of many waters; He
> had in His right hand seven stars, out of His mouth went a sharp
> two-edged sword, and His countenance was like the sun shining in

its strength. **And when I saw Him, I fell at His feet as dead.** But He laid His right hand on me, saying to me, "Do not be afraid; I am the First and the Last." (Revelation 1:12–17, emphasis added)

When we read the book of Revelation, we discover that Jesus is returning for His Bride to settle the score and take back this planet from the kingdom of darkness. There will be no cross in His future, no suffering for lost humanity. He will return in glory to judge and to conquer. He will return as Messiah ben David, the conquering King and the wrath of God personified. The Apostle Paul declares:

For the mystery of lawlessness is already at work; only He who now restrains will do so until He is taken out of the way. And then the lawless one will be revealed, **whom the Lord will consume with the breath of His mouth and destroy with the brightness of His coming.** (2 Thessalonians 2:7–8, emphasis added)

The same vortex of splendor that has the angels in Heaven crying out, "holy, holy, holy" will vaporize the son of perdition (and his armies) at Jesus' return.

May God open our eyes and hearts to realize God's absolute splendor and holiness. If we could get but a glimpse, we would be forever changed.

If we can wrap our minds around this truth of the greatness of God and how the universe is not significant enough to contain Him, then our minds are blown away by the Paul's declaration:

For in Him dwells all the fullness of the Godhead bodily. (Colossians 2:9)

We have yet to grasp the power of the incarnation of Christ. What the universe and all three heavens could not contain walked among people, and the apostles proclaimed, "Immanuel" (God is with us)! The very thought of the incarnation humbles me and brings me to tears. The more I learn about God, the more I tremble. Like David, I want to proclaim:

> When I consider Your heavens, the work of Your fingers, The moon and the stars, which You have ordained, What is man that You are mindful of him, And the son of man that You visit him? For You have made him a little lower than the angels, And You have crowned him with glory and honor. You have made him to have dominion over the works of Your hands; You have put all things under his feet, (Psalm 8:3–6)

As I write this chapter, there is a tug on my heart. The more I discover about God in His Word, and the more the Holy Spirit draws me closer to my Savior, the force of that tug increases. That tug is the gravity of the vortex of splendor that surrounds the throne of God. One day, I will be entirely captured by this supernatural gravity as well. I will not be able to stand. On that day, I will bow down before the throne in Heaven and proclaim His greatness. The Kingdom warrior has experienced the weight of the presence of God and has been touched by the Almighty's splendor. How could Hell frighten a warrior who has experienced the manifested presence of the Holy God? What could ever tempt a warrior to abandon what he knows is his future in Heaven for the tarnished things of this world?

I must confess I have a problem with some individuals who claim to be prophets in our day who seem to make daily trips to Heaven, yet there is no fear of the LORD in them. Only a handful of times has God given me a glimpse of Heaven, just mere moments of vision. Those moments of glory have rattled me to my core. They are so profound and so holy that they're not easily shared. As I wrote this chapter, thinking about them has reduced me to sobbing several times uncontrollably. I wish I could show them to you and make you understand. But how can

you describe the indescribable? The Psalmist calls us to a divine appointment to personally experience the LORD.

> The angel of the LORD encamps all around those who fear Him,
> and delivers them. Oh, taste and see that the LORD is good;
> blessed is the man who trusts in Him! Oh, fear the LORD, you
> His saints! There is no want to those who fear Him. The young
> lions lack and suffer hunger; but those who seek the LORD shall
> not lack any good thing. (Psalm 34:7–10)

We need to ask the Holy Spirit to teach us the fear of the LORD.
That fear of the LORD is essential "Basic Kingdom Warrior 101." We
cannot graduate from boot camp without it. Just look at the promises
in Psalm 34 for those who fear the LORD. These promises alone should
have us crying out daily for the Holy Spirit to instill within us the fear
of God.

A quote from Isaiah chapter 33 seems to speak to the time that is
quickly approaching the Remnant.

> The LORD is exalted, for He dwells on high; He has filled Zion
> with justice and righteousness. Wisdom and knowledge will be
> the stability of your times, and the strength of salvation; the fear
> of the LORD is His treasure. (Isaiah 33:5–6)

The Word tells us that the beginning of wisdom and knowledge
are found in the fear of the LORD. In the fear of the LORD, we will find
stability in the times ahead.

The fear of the LORD is an essential building block in the warrior's
wall of protection. This essential block must be laid directly against the
Cornerstone (Jesus). If we do not add the fear of God next to our great
Cornerstone, we will be out of alignment with the Kingdom of God. At
best, the pressure of the world around us will skew our perception and

cause us to miss the mark as true Kingdom warriors. At worst, we will be deceived into fighting the enemies' battles for them and wound the people of God around us.

It isn't insignificant that, while we're admonished to "fear not" 365 times in the Bible (which always refers to the situations of life), we're instructed to "fear God" 490 times!

Here is a quick list.

✣ The fear of God—84 times.
✣ Fear of God—86 times.
✣ The fear of the LORD—186 times.
✣ Fear God—134 times.
✣ A total of 490 times.[93]

Did you know one of the things that separated Messiah from everyone else was His expertise in moving in the fear of the LORD? The prophet Isaiah declared:

> There shall come forth a Rod from the stem of Jesse, and a Branch shall grow out of his roots. The Spirit of the LORD shall rest upon Him, the Spirit of wisdom and understanding, the Spirit of counsel and might, the Spirit of knowledge and of the fear of the LORD. His delight is in the fear of the LORD, and He shall not judge by the sight of His eyes, nor decide by the hearing of His ears. (Isaiah 11:1–3)

In Scripture, when we see a word or phrase used repeatedly, it is the Hebraic way of emphasizing its importance. For example, when Isaiah revealed the seven anointings of Messiah (also called the "seven aspects of the Holy Spirit"), he placed the fear of the LORD above all the other six. In verse 3, the KJV states Jesus would be "of quick understanding in the fear of the LORD." *A Commentary: Critical, Experimental, and Prac-*

tical on the Old and New Testaments provides further insight into what "quick understanding" means.

Verse 3. make him of quick understanding—literally, "*quick-scented* in the fear of Jehovah"; endowed with a singular sagacity in discerning the genuine principle of religious fear of God, when it lies dormant in the yet unawakened sinner (Mt 12:20 Ac 10; Ac 16:14).[94]

"Sagacity" as mentioned in this definition is no longer a common word in our modern vocabulary. The word means "one that possesses keen wisdom, understanding, judgment, deep insight, intelligence, and acuity." As our example, Jesus moved in an unprecedented level of the fear of the LORD. This deep respect for the will and purposes of the Father was the driving force in everything that He did. Kingdom warriors must follow the example of our King. The fear of the LORD is essential to remaining faithful in purpose and immune to the enemy's mind games.

The Fear of the LORD and Humility

Brethren, if a man is overtaken in any trespass, you who are spiritual restore such a one in a spirit of gentleness, considering yourself lest you also be tempted. (Galatians 6:1)

Kingdom warriors who walk in the fear of the LORD resist the prideful thought that they are beyond temptation. As long as we are in this world, we must guard against the enemy's tactics. I've learned over the years that the kingdom of darkness adapts quickly (while God's people are usually as slow as molasses running uphill on a cold winter's day). Evaluating, adapting, and overcoming are paramount to Kingdom warriors' successes on the battlefield. We must always be watchful for the enemy, as he will always be trying new things to tempt us.

The Kingdom Warrior is also aware that there may be blind spots while establishing the perimeter. During the Vietnam War, the North Vietnamese, backed by the Soviet Union and China, had established an underground network of tunnels throughout the land. Pop-up attacks against US-supported South Vietnam could occur without warning and would seem to come from nowhere. One of the most powerful prayers the Holy Spirit has given my dear wife, Mary, is pleading for the protection of the blood of Jesus over any doors the enemy has opened in her life that she's unaware of. She then asks the Holy Spirit to point out those doors so she can take care of them. I learned from Mary's example and began to pray the same way. Some doors may be such things about unforgiveness about situations we've have long forgotten or unresolved problems we need to take care of. (I cannot tell you how often that has happened to me.) Other doors may be secular traditions that have crept into our belief system—activities that didn't originate in the Word of God but that have tentacles leading back to Babylon. When we earnestly pray this type of prayer, we must be ready for the Holy Spirit to move. We should respond with readiness to quickly repent of our sin, resolve any problems those sins have created, research what God's Word says about the issue, and then change our behavior accordingly. Remember, we must continually evaluate, adapt, and overcome while we're on the battlefields of life.

Now, let's return to the words of the Apostle Peter:

> Be sober, be vigilant; because your adversary the devil walks about like a roaring lion, seeking whom he may devour. (1 Peter 5:8)

If we could create a military patch for Kingdom warriors that would encapsulate the spirit of this end-time force, it would have two phrases emblazed upon it: "Always Faithful" and "Always Vigilant."

May the fire of God burn these truths deep within your heart.

As we approach the return of our conquering King, the enemy will pull out every stop in his endgame strategies. As this happens, the activity on the battlefield will evolve quickly. It will develop so rapidly that the masses will be swept up in its complexity and hellish brilliance. Therefore, it is imperative that Kingdom warriors secure the perimeter now in order to be ready for the fast-approaching day.

And do this, knowing the time, that now it is high time to awake out of sleep; for now our salvation is nearer than when we first believed. The night is far spent, the day is at hand. Therefore let us cast off the works of darkness, and let us put on the armor of light. (Romans 13:11–12)

Prayer

Father, please teach me the fear of the LORD. Then, like Moses, I ask you to show me your glory. Let me be like Jesus, and let my primary response to all things be in fear of you.

I now plead the blood of Jesus over every door in my life, especially those I cannot see. Let the blood be a barrier to the enemy and then reveal these doors to me. Then, give me your grace to close these doors and establish my Kingdom perimeter permanently.

I ask that your Spirit would always assist me in remaining vigilant. Help me evaluate, adapt, and overcome the enemy's tactics and win souls for your Kingdom, in Jesus' name.

Review Questions

1. In your own words, describe the fear of the LORD.
2. Why is personal holiness so crucial for the Kingdom warriors?
3. Why is the incarnation of Christ so amazing?
4. Why is the book of Revelation considered the fourth Gospel?
5. How is Isaiah 33:5–6 connected to the end times?
6. Jesus is the Cornerstone of our faith. What stone must be laid directly against the Cornerstone in order for Kingdom warriors to maintain biblical balance?
7. Why is pleading for the protection of the blood of Jesus over the doors we cannot see so important?
8. Why is "vigilance" a watchword for Kingdom warriors in the last days?

USE THE QR-CODE BELOW TO
ACCESS MANY SPECIAL DEALS AND
PROMOTIONS ON BOOKS AND FILMS
FEATURING DISCOVERY, PROPHECY,
AND THE SUPERNATURAL!

NOTES

1. John N. Oswalt, "Book of Isaiah, Chapters 1–39," *New International Commentary on the Old Testament* (Grand Rapids, MI: Eerdmans, 1986), 454–455.

2. Strong's G# 04102. *Strong's Enhanced Lexicon*. BibleWorks for Windows 10.0. BibleWorks, LLC, (Norfolk, VA, 2015).

3. Michael K. Lake, *The Kingdom Priesthood: Preparing and Equipping the Remnant Priesthood for the Last Days*. (Seymour, MO: Biblical Life Publishing, 2020), 94.

4. Barclay M. Newman Jr., *A Concise Greek-English Dictionary of the New Testament*. (Stuttgart, Germany: *Deutsche Bibelgesellschaft*; United Bible Societies, 1993), 62.

5. William Arndt, et al., *A Greek-English Lexicon of the New Testament and Other Early Christian Literature* (Chicago: University of Chicago Press, 2000), 672.

6. Robert H. Mounce, *The Book of Revelation*, (Grand Rapids, MI: Wm. B. Eerdmans Publishing Co., 1997), WORD*search* CROSS e-book, 326.

7. Daniel Bates, "Jeffrey Epstein Shipped $100K Cement Truck to 'Pedophile Island' Three Weeks before Damning Expose Was

Released, Paying for Machine up Front so It Would Arrive Quicker, as Experts Say He Could Have 'Literally Covered up Evidence,'" *Daily Mail*, https://www.dailymail.co.uk/news/article-7361297/Jeffrey-Epstein-shipped-50K-cement-truck-Pedophile-Island-cover-evidence.html?ico=pushly-notifcation-small.

8. Vigilant Citizen, "Burying Tunnels? Epstein Had $100,000 of Cement Delivered to His Island Before His Arrest." https://vigilantcitizen.com/latestnews/burying-tunnels-epstein-delivered-100000-of-cement-delivered-to-his-island-before-his-arrest/.

9. Jia Tolentio, "Is Abortion Sacred?" *New Yorker*, https://www.newyorker.com/culture/essay/is-abortion-sacred.

10. Strong's G#1127.

11. Strong's #G2675.

12. William D. Mounce, *Mounce's Complete Expository Dictionary of Old & New Testament Words* (Grand Rapids, MI: Zondervan, 2006), 1184.

13. William Arndt, et al., *A Greek-English Lexicon of the New Testament and Other Early Christian Literature* (Chicago: University of Chicago Press, 2000), 945.

14. Strong's G# 3958.

15. Strong's #G 2311.

16. Faithlife / Logos Bible Software, 2014.

17. William Arndt, et al., *A Greek-English Lexicon of the New Testament and Other Early Christian Literature* (Chicago: University of Chicago Press, 2000), 782.

18. Faithlife / Logos Bible Software, 2014.

19. Strong's H# 2617.

20. Ibid.

21. Strong's H# 2580.

22. Strong's G#5485.

23. Ibid.

24. Henry George Liddell, et al., *A Greek-English Lexicon* (Oxford: Clarendon Press, 1996), 1979.

25. Strong's G# 1656.

26. I use *Yahweh* as the pronunciation of *YHVH* in the Hebrew. This is the most recognized and used form of pronouncing the tetragrammaton within Christian literature. Ancient Hebrew did not possess the vowel points that it has today, and the exact way of pronouncing *YHVH* has been lost in the mists of time. Leading experts within the field of biblical Hebrew have settled on about four distinct ways of pronouncing this sacred name. *Yahweh* is but one of them. Its use in this book is neither intended to endorse a position nor offend anyone. I am simply addressing my targeted audience of Gentile believers.

27. Abraham Cohen, *Everyman's Talmud: The Major Teachings of the Rabbinic Sages* (New York: Schocken Books, 1949) 17.

28. I. Howard Marshall, "The Epistles of John," *The New International Commentary on the New Testament* (Grand Rapids, MI: Eerdmans, 1978), 101–102.

29. Jon Brown, "Sermon about Jesus' 'Trans Body' and 'Vaginal' Side Wound Shocks Churchgoers Who Shout 'Heresy'," *New York Post*, https://nypost.com/2022/11/27/sermon-about-jesus-trans-body-and-vaginal-side-wound-shocks-churchgoers-who-shout-heresy/.

30. Strong's G# 1849.

31. Strong's H#02999.

32. Strong's H#02390.

33. Strong's H#03478.

34. Paul Barnett, *The Second Epistle to the Corinthians, The New International Commentary on the New Testament* (Grand Rapids, MI: Eerdmans, 1997), 570.

35. Ibid.

36. John Klein and Adam Spears, *Lost in Translation Volume 1: Rediscovering the Hebrew Roots of Our Faith* (Bend, OR: Selah Publishing Group, 2007, 2014, 2016). 68.

37. R. Laird Harris, Gleason L. Archer, Bruce K. Waltke, ed., "910: יָרָה," in *Theological Wordbook of the Old Testament* (Chicago: Moody Press, 1980), WORD*search* CROSS e-book, 404.

38. Dr. Ron Mosley, *Yeshua: A Guide to the Real Jesus and the Original Church* (Messianic Jewish Communications. Kindle Edition), 56–57.

39. Strong's G#03551.

40. "What Does Lex Mean in Latin Article?" https://www.wordhippo.com/what-is/the-meaning-of/latin-word-d1f3732a9a6a6d5ae438388e1df2164bdb35d371.html.

41. Note: When referring to the Roman Catholic Church, I prefer to use the term "Christendom" rather than "Church", to separate the two in the minds of my readers.

42. Note: In Jewish literature, Maimonides can also be referred to as Maimon and RaMBaM.

43. https://en.wikipedia.org/wiki/Mishneh_Torah.

44. Strong's #G458.

45. Strong's #G1381.

46. Douglas J. Moo, "Epistle to the Romans," *New International Commentary on the New Testament* (Grand Rapids, MI: Eerdmans, 1996), 756–757.

47. Strong's #G3137.

48. Strong's #G3148.

49. One for Israel, https://www.oneforisrael.org/holidays/tisha-bav/.

50. "What Is Spiritual adultery?" http://www.gotquestions.org/spiritual-adultery.html.

51. Daniel Isaac Block, "The Book of Ezekiel, Chapters 1–24," *New International Commentary on the Old Testament* (Grand Rapids, MI: Eerdmans, 1997), 558–559.

52. Michael Lake, *The Shinar Directive: Preparing the Way for the Son of Perdition's Return* (Crane, MO: Defender; Kindle Edition), 61.

53. Strong's #H02254.

54. Strong's #G1319.

55. Strong's #G1849.

56. Neil Anderson, "Defeating Satan's Footholds and Strongholds," https://preachitteachit.org/articles/detail/defeating-satans-footholds-and-strongholds/.

57. In the KJV, *kai* is translated as "as" 342 times, "when" 42 times, "how" 18 times, "as it were" 20 times, and "about" 14 times. How it is translated depends quite a bit on context and the one doing the interpretation. In light of the parable of Matthew 18, if *kai* could be translated as "when" in the Lord's Prayer, it would have a dynamic impact upon the believer.

58. Strong's #G03875.

59. William Schnoebelen, *Exposing the Illuminati from Within*, Video. Prophecy Club, Topeka, Kansas.

60. Regan Olsson, "Birth to 5 Years: Updates to Your Child's Developmental Milestones," https://www.bannerhealth.com/healthcareblog/teach-me/birth-to-five-years-knowing-your-childs-developmental-milestones.

61. Rick Renner, D*ressed to Kill: A Biblical Approach to Spiritual Warfare and Armor*. (Harrison House Publishers; Kindle Edition).

62. Henry George Liddell, et al., *A Greek-English Lexicon* (Oxford: Clarendon Press, 1996), 453.

63. Strong's H#08414.

64. Strong's G#0225.

65. Adam Clarke, *Adam Clarke's Commentary*, (New York: Abingdon-Cokesbury, 1826), WORD*search* CROSS e-book, "Hebrews."

66. Strong's G#1319.

67. Finis Jennings Dake, *Dake's Annotated Reference Bible: Containing the Old and New Testaments of the Authorized or King James Version Text* (Lawrenceville, GA: Dake Bible Sales, 1997), WORDsearch CROSS e-book, chapter 2.

68. Ibid., chapter 5.

69. Ibid., chapter 2.

70. https://www.brainyquote.com/authors/george-bernard-shaw-quotes.

71. https://www.brainyquote.com/quotes/vladimir_lenin_136421?src=t_socialism.

72. https://www.brainyquote.com/quotes/

herbert_spencer_380078?src=t_socialism.

73. Robert Sepehr, *Redemption Through Sin: Global Conspiracy in History, Religion, Politics and Finance.* (Atlantean Gardens, 1666 Kindle Edition).

74. Ibid.

75. Ibid.

76. Ibid.

77. Ibid.

78. Gershom Scholem, *The Messianic Idea in Judaism* (Knopf Doubleday, Kindle Edition), 127.

79. Ibid.

80. Ibid., 129–130.

81. Ibid., 131–132.

82. Joseph Trainor, *Illuminati News,* "New World Order and Utopian Globalism," http://www.illuminati-news.com/adam-weishaupt.htm.

83. John Carter, *Sex and Rockets: The Occult World of Jack Parsons* (Kindle Edition) 156–159).

84. Will Graham, "Ten Concerns That Francis Shaeffer Took to His Grave," Evangelical Focus Europe, https://evangelicalfocus.com/fresh-breeze/2383/10-concerns-francis-schaeffer-took-to-the-grave

85. Michael J. Norton, *Field Guide to Spiritual Warfare: Pull the Impossible* (Shippensburg, PA: Destiny Image, 2011).

86. Strong's G#0283.

87. What Does Hebrews 13:4 Mean? https://www.gotquestions.org/marriage-bed-undefiled.html.

88. John Eckhardt, *Deliverance and Spiritual Warfare Manual* (Lake Mary, FL: Charisma House, 2014), 237.

89. Ibid., 29–30.

90. Clarke, *Adam Clarke's Commentary,* "1 Corinthians."

91. *New American Standard Bible: 1995 Update* (La Habra, CA: Lockman Foundation, 1995), 2 Corinthians 6:14.

92. Clarke, *Adam Clarke's Commentary,* "John."

93. https://www.answers.com/Q/
How_many_times_is_the_fear_of_god_mentioned_in_the_bible.
94. Robert Jamieson, A. R. Fausset, David Brown, *A Commentary: Critical, Experimental, and Practical on the Old and New Testaments*, (Toledo, OH: Jerome B. Names 1884), WORD*search* CROSS e-book, "Chapter 11."